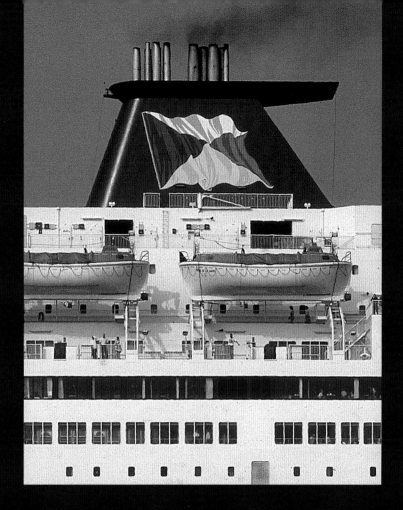

P&O Ferries

THROUGH FIVE DECADES

John Hendy Miles Cowsill

PRIDE OF HULL

P&O

Rob de Visser

Ferry
Publications

Published by:
Ferry Publications, PO Box 33, Ramsey, Isle of Man IM99 4LP
Tel: +44 (0) 1624 898445   Fax: +44 (0) 1624 898449
E-mail: ferrypubs@manx.net   Website: www.ferrypubs.co.uk

Contents

Foreword 4

Introduction 6

1   The Dover Story.. 8

2   The Normandy & Iberian routes 52

3   The North Sea Connections...82

4   Linking the UK with Ireland 110

5   P&O Scottish Ferries heritage routes 136

P&O Fleet List 144

Produced and designed by Ferry Publications trading as Lily Publications Ltd

PO Box 33, Ramsey, Isle of Man, British Isles, IM99 4LP

Tel: +44 (0) 1624 898446   Fax: +44 (0) 1624 898449

www.ferrypubs.co.uk E-Mail: info@lilypublications.co.uk

Printed and bound by Gomer Press Ltd., Wales, UK +44 (0) 1559 362371 © Lily Publications 2012

Foreword

BY HELEN DEEBLE

As chief executive of P&O Ferries it gives me great pleasure to introduce to you the compelling story of our company and its place in the shipping industry through the pages of this carefully researched book.

Today P&O Ferries operates a mixed fleet of more than 20 ships in most of the principal shipping corridors around the British Isles and we are proud to offer round the clock services to our freight and tourist customers.

We do this with a modern fleet that is largely purpose designed for the job and our ships include some of the largest and most luxurious ferries in the world.

Ours is a dynamic and ever-changing business that traces its history to the early days of modern cross-Channel travel in the 1920s and it incorporates some fascinating stories of entrepreneurship and visionary thinking along the way.

This book is a tribute to the people who have designed, built and operated these vessels over the years.

Helen Deeble
Chief Executive   P&O Ferries

Introduction

To mark the 175th anniversary of the founding of P&O, this book traces the history of P&O Ferries which is a comparatively recent amalgamation of a number of separate concerns which were later acquired by the company.

Historically, three visionary shipping entrepreneurs were to contribute to the company's success and their quite different business strategies later grew, developed and flourished under the wing of the European Ferries Group (EFG).

At Dover, Stuart Townsend started a motorists' service to Calais using a small, chartered collier in 1928. Two years later his Townsend Bros Car Ferries Ltd converted a redundant minelayer and provided a stern door for future drive-on operations. Under the later ownership of George Nott Industries and then the EFG, led by the energetic Roland Wickenden and later by his brother Keith, the company flourished and became the English Channel's principal operator. During the same period the nationalised ferry company was being stifled by Government constraints and concerns over the building of a tunnel beneath the Channel.

Then there was Lt. Col. Frank Bustard whose the Atlantic Steam Navigation Company pioneered the first roll on – roll off service for freight across both the Irish Sea and the southern North Sea and who later introduced the world's first purpose-built ro-ro vessel. Although his initial vision was for a cut-price trans-Atlantic service, his World War Two service in the army, preparing vessels for the D-Day landings, made him aware of the tremendous potential of the roll on – roll off concept on which he later fully capitalised.

The third ferry industry pioneer was the Norwegian ship owner Otto Thoresen who commenced the first UK - France drive-through service with his revolutionary multi-purpose ships (for passengers, cars and freight) from Southampton in

*The **European Causeway** arrives in Loch Ryan from Northern Ireland. (Gordon Hislip)*

1964. He showed that modern, attractive and efficient ships could make profits on loss-making routes in spite of the gloomy forecasts of the nationalised railway company who saw no future in their own cross-Channel services from the Hampshire port.

Today P&O Ferries concentrate their business in three key areas: the Dover Strait, Irish Sea and North Sea although the company's own ferry operations were not established until the 1960s. Under the guidance of Ian Churcher, the overnight Hull – Rotterdam link succeeded and flourished in spite of the worst fears of many industry analysts. At Southampton, the P&O subsidiary company Normandy Ferries introduced the Anglo-French Le Havre link while Dover to Boulogne was added to the English Channel services in 1976. This continued

crossing between Cairnryan and Larne which had, for historical reasons, previously been linked with operations at Felixstowe.

The North Sea Ferries links from Hull and later Teesport were unaffected by these changes as they were 50% owned by the Dutch company Royal Nedlloyd. However, in 1996, P&O gained complete control over the company after which P&O North Sea Ferries was formed and the ships were also rebranded.

Difficult trading conditions and increased competition sadly saw a contraction of operations with services from Mostyn, Felixstowe and Fleetwood being sold between 2002 and 2004, and with the lack of investment in new tonnage, the Portsmouth cross-Channel operations also ceased in 2005.

In December 2005, the P&O Group was sold to Dubai Ports World (DPW) for £3.33 billion and so ended 168 years of independence. Although DPW were primarily interested in the acquisition of container ports, for P&O Ferries the takeover represented a new era in which the English Channel's largest ferries, the 47,000 gross ton twins *Spirit of Britain* and *Spirit of France* entered service in 2011/12, setting new standards and expectations on the premier Dover – Calais route.

With unprecedented competition, a world recession and overcapacity on many routes, a further business review takes place in 2012 when there will doubtless be further changes to P&O Ferries. Whatever the outcome, we may be certain that the company will continue to make every effort to both maintain and improve its existing services whilst adapting them to suit the ever-changing market conditions in an extremely demanding economic climate.

John Hendy & Miles Cowsill
September 2012

until the ageing P&O Normandy Ferries fleet was sold to the EFG (trading as Townsend Thoresen) in 1985. Efforts had also been made to establish links to Spain, Portugal and north Africa under the auspices of another subsidiary company, Southern Ferries.

In late 1986, the EFG was absorbed by the P&O Group and in the following October P&O European Ferries was born. The acquisition involved ships and passenger services from Felixstowe, Dover, Portsmouth and Cairnryan in addition to a number of purely freight routes.

In the Irish Sea sector, P&O began their operations in 1974 when they founded Pandoro to operate a freight service to Ireland. Expansion followed but in 1998 the company was rebranded P&O Irish Sea, also taking in the North Channel

Chapter 1

The Dover Story

ORIGINS

The origins of the P&O operation we see today go back over 100 years and involve a complete transport revolution and a total re-emphasis in the development of both Dover and Calais ports.

The very first car to have been carried by ship across the English Channel was transported in the hold of the South Eastern & Chatham Railway's turbine steamer *Onward* between Folkestone and Boulogne in 1904. Two years later, a young 19-year-old Stuart Townsend made his first tour of Spain when his father's car had to be shipped out from England in crates, finally arriving at its destination to be assembled three weeks later. Frequent motoring holidays led the young Townsend to believe that this archaic system of shipping motor vehicles across the English Channel could certainly be improved upon.

By 1911 transporting vehicles across the Channel had become commonplace and the new Dover-Calais steamers *Engadine* and *Riviera* were fitted with specially strengthened decks for the carriage of motor cars. The method of loading cars was by crane in the time-honoured lift on–lift off method and the success, or otherwise, depended on the pinpoint accuracy of the crane operator whose demanding job it was to lift the car from the quayside and swing it across onto the decks or into the hold of the adjacent ship. There was not much margin for error during this tricky operation which was made even more difficult during periods of strong wind when, once airborne, the precious car would swing about and might be damaged by landing too heavily on a pitching deck. Watching one's car being loaded in those days must have been a constant cause for concern for anxious motorists.

In 1923, following the First World War, the Southern Railway Company was formed and took over the British operation of cross-Channel shipping from Dover. The company management held the view that as motorists must be wealthy people, they could be charged on the principle of what the traffic would stand. Cars were frequently damaged in transit and owners were often pestered by the loading gangs whose palms appeared to be constantly open. In addition, at that time the Board of Trade did not permit cars to carry petrol during

shipment and many gallons of fuel ended up in the sea. An experienced driver might arrive at his port of embarkation with his petrol tank all but empty but occasionally things could go wrong. Stuart Townsend remembered the time when his car ground to a halt just outside Boulogne and required the services of a strong horse to pull it to the quayside.

Townsend Bros Shipping Ltd had been founded in 1889 with their main business in ship delivery, management and forwarding. In 1927, at the age of 40, Stuart Townsend undertook a feasibility study into a projected new service linking Dover and Calais and found that it was possible to undercut the Southern Railway's car rates by 50 per cent and yet still make a small profit. In order to make any new service pay, a guarantee of ten cars a day for a month was required and the backing of the motoring organisations was duly sought. Sadly both the RAC and the AA declined to assist but the editor of 'The Autocar' magazine and the secretary of the Civil Service Motoring Association were both most helpful and with their backing Townsend, to use his own words, "took the plunge!"

In those days, everyone knew Stuart Townsend as 'Captain' Townsend. However, he was not a Master Mariner as this was a title that he had gained when in the army during the First World War and, along with many others who held this rank, was retained during the 1920s and 30s. His next task was to find a suitable ship and Townsend Bros Shipping Ltd duly chartered the small 386 gross tons, coastal collier *Artificer* which was owned by 'T' Steam Coasters of Newcastle. The vessel was similar in size and design to many other small coal-carrying ships of this period; she had been built as the *Mercury* in Dundee during 1905 and had passed to her new owners in 1914. Initially the charter was for a period of just one month but, just in case the service proved to be a success, an option for a second month was made.

Townsend's service commenced in July 1928 using a berth tucked out of the way in the Camber at Dover's Eastern Docks which was, during that period, mainly involved in a flourishing ship breaking business. The focus and centre of the port's cross-Channel trade was the Admiralty Pier at the Western Docks and its splendid new Marine Station from which the gleaming London bound Continental Boat Expresses would commence their brisk sprint through Kent to the capital. At that time there were no commercial shipping operations from the Camber.

On the French side, the service operated from the Quay Paul Devot on the opposite side of the harbour from the Gare Maritime and the passenger ship berths. Rates for the new service were £2 single and £3.15s (£3.75) return for vehicles up to 8 ft 6 in. long – this against the £5.15s (£5.75) single fare of the railway company.

Townsend reasoned that it would take the Southern Railway one month to understand what he was doing and a second month to do something about it. His aim was simple; to force the Southern to reduce their rates and then cease trading.

The new entrepreneurial Townsend service was the easyJet of its generation – a cheap, cheerful and no frills operation. However, the tiny *Artificer* frequently ran with a full load of 15 cars and 12 passengers but Townsend was struck by the number of motorists expressing a wish to travel with their vehicles. Passengers in excess of 12 were taken by motor coach to the Admiralty Pier and crossed to Calais via the Southern Railway's passenger steamer. For many this was an unpopular move as the majority preferred to remain with their cars, even though the *Artificer*'s crossing time was a whole 2 hours 30 minutes during a period when the Southern's service took just an hour. Facilities on board the *Artificer* were basic to say the least and if food was required then motorists would have to make their own arrangements with the ship's cook.

From the very start of the new motorists' service, Townsend enjoyed excellent relationships with Dover Harbour Board, whose Chairman Sir William Crundall had an ongoing feud with the Southern's Sir Herbert Walker, and also with the Calais Chamber of Commerce which welcomed the new service with open arms.

With the *Artificer* not being available for the 1929 season, another Newcastle-based collier was chartered. This was the Border Shipping Co's *Royal Firth* (411 gross tons) which had been built at Hull in 1921. The year also marked the formation of Townsend Bros Car Ferries whose first directors were appointed on 13th March. Profit for the first year's operation was £80!

The Southern Railway's response to Townsend's new service was to introduce their own service for car owners, both on the Dover-Calais and Folkestone-Boulogne routes, firstly charging the same rates and then undercutting them in an attempt to see off the newcomer. In spite of this, traffic remained buoyant but it was obvious that there was not enough for both operators to continue throughout the winter and so during the autumn, the Townsend service was suspended. A more permanent response came in May 1930 when the Southern introduced its own car ferry, the *Autocarrier* (35 cars, 120 passengers).

ENTER THE FORDE

The Townsend board had realised by this time that if the service was to continue then it was no longer satisfactory to source spare colliers for summer use as car ferries; a permanent ship was required which in addition to carrying a good number of cars could also accommodate passengers. As it happened, they did not have far to look as in Dover's Eastern Docks, the former Royal Navy 'Town' class minesweeper HMS *Ford* was waiting to be scrapped. After inspection, the vessel was purchased for £5,000 and was duly sent to Messrs Earle's Shipbuilding & Engineering Co. of Hull where she was stripped and converted for civilian use.

HMS *Ford* had been built in 1919 by Dunlop Bremner & Co. of Port Glasgow but had seen little service under the White Ensign and was therefore in particularly good order. The ship measured 231 ft overall with a beam of 28 ft 6 in. and was converted for £14,000 under the design of Norman M. Dewar. Several vessels of this type had already been taken up for merchant trade but this was the first instance where one of them was required to carry a Steam 2 passenger certificate for short international voyages. On examination, her hull was found to be in excellent condition and although she was built with more than enough bulkheads for cross-Channel trade, and some were removed, the strength of the remainder had to be increased to satisfy the watchful eye of the Board of Trade. In order to allow cars to carry petrol in their tanks for the first time, the vessel's new car deck was constructed of steel.

As a height of 7 ft 6 in. was required between the car and boat decks, the whole of the minesweeper's accommodation was replaced. At one stage extending the boat deck to the stern was considered but this idea was abandoned due to concerns over the ship's stability. In any case, she would already offer plenty of outside deck space and there was always the chance that high-sided vehicles or buses might be attracted to the service.

Heavy belting was constructed around the hull to protect it from routine knocks and scrapes within the confines of Dover and Calais harbours. Being a former naval vessel there was little in the way of astern power and there was no bow rudder for running astern. Bow thrust units – standard fittings on all modern ferries – were unheard of then.

A passenger certificate was awarded for 168 passengers and 34 crew although additional passengers could be carried under a Steam 2 Limited Certificate for daylight service under ten hours' duration meaning 307 people could be carried. There was enough space for approximately 28 cars which could turn round on the 26 ft wide vehicle deck if required. Accommodation was plain but comfortable with a smoke room, a ladies room, a large general saloon and three private state cabins.

The ship remained coal burning although it was hoped that at some stage in the future she might be converted to oil. It was also hoped that it might soon be possible to avoid the lift on–lift off process by installing a special 9 ft x 6 ft door at the vessel's stern in order that it might flap down onto specially constructed bridges which would link the quay with the ship. The reluctance of harbour authorities, the Board of Trade and the intervention of the Second World War saw the roll on–roll off principle stagnate for another 21 years.

As there was already a ship in merchant service with the same name, hers was amended simply by adding an 'E' so that Ford became the Forde and, as such, she commenced commercial service on 15th April 1930.

Services were daily leaving Dover at 11.30, arriving at Calais at 13.00 and leaving again two hours later. Tariffs remained the same as they were two years previously, the only difference being that in order to enjoy the greatly superior accommodation, passengers were charged an extra 2s (10p).

At a special lunch in the Hotel Continental in Calais, Stuart Townsend remarked that motorists would still prefer to drive their vehicles on board and that it was hoped to have a special

*The chartered collier **Artificer** commenced the Townsend Channel Ferry service in 1928. (Ferry Publications Library)*

gangway working at Dover that year while arrangements on the French side would not be in use until 1931. Sadly, neither of these schemes came into fruition until after the war.

The motoring public certainly liked the Forde and the service she offered and traffic grew in leaps and bounds. The 1931 season started as early as 30th March and during the thirties, so many availed themselves of the Townsend ferry that it was common practice to charter coasters to handle extra cars while the Forde absorbed all the passengers. The Southern Railway continued to undercut Townsend's rates but in 1937 they were finally admitted to the 'pool' operated by the other ferry users and rates were restored to a commercial basis.

ROLL ON

On 9th June 1936, a three-week General Strike started in France. For Townsend this meant that at Calais there was no one to work the crane to lift off and lift on the Forde's cars. The shipping world then witnessed just how fast and simple the roll on–roll off method of loading was when, at the correct

*Top: Leaving Calais in the **Forde**. Of particular interest is her stern door which was only used during the French General Strike of 1936. (A.D. Townsend)*

*Above: A post-war view of the **Forde** leaving Dover for Calais without her distinctive funnel cowl. (A.D. Townsend)*

level of the tide, the *Forde* presented her stern to the Calais quayside, lowered her stern gate and discharged in minutes. No one who witnessed this operation could have failed to be impressed and Townsend's dream of a roll on–roll off service would have most certainly gathered momentum had it not been for the intervention of the war.

By now it was already becoming evident that the *Forde* was finding it increasingly difficult to cope with all the traffic on offer and in July 1936 she was offered for sale while Townsend looked for a larger replacement. Norman Dewar even drew up plans for a traditional-looking new ship but with an ugly hoistable ramp situated at the after end which would have effectively allowed cars to load at any state of the tide.

Three years later, the Larvik-Frederikshavn ferry *Peter Wessel* was inspected but although the Norwegian ferry was of an advanced design with headroom for lorries and drive-through facilities, it was felt that as her owners always ran her at full speed, her engines might give trouble and interest in her waned. The Board of Trade had previously made it known that had such a ship been introduced on the Dover-Calais route, then the bow door would have to be welded shut and it was not until 1965 that Britain's first drive-through ferry, the *Free Enterprise II* finally entered service.

At the outbreak of war, Townsend sent the *Forde* to lay up in Poole Harbour where he could keep an eye on her from his nearby cottage at Sandbanks. The ship was finally requisitioned in October 1939 and served throughout the period of hostilities as a salvage vessel. Being of light construction, she was not ideal for this role and appears to have enjoyed a quiet war.

The Royal Navy finally pulled out of Dover in December 1946 and on the following 1st April, Townsend was back in business using the coaster *Cromarty Firth* (588 gross tons, built in 1937) for a three-week period before the *Forde* returned from refit at Southampton. With post-war travelling restrictions lifted in 1948, cross-Channel car ferry trade dramatically increased with both the Southern Railway and Belgian Marine introducing larger tonnage to carry this specialised traffic.

The *Forde* was finally retired from service on 18th October 1949 when she was sent to lay up in London. The following month came her sale for £20,000 to MH Bland of Gibraltar for the ferry service linking Gibraltar with Tangier. As the *Gibel Tarik* she continued in service until in September 1953 when her boilers finally failed and she was scrapped in Malaga in the following March. During this latter period in service, the ship starred in a comedy film with Alec Guiness called 'The Captain's Paradise' in which Guiness played the role of the ship's Master with a wife in both ports.

THE HALLADALE

During 1947, Stuart Townsend's son David had joined the company as the Manager at Dover. He had served in the Royal Navy during the war and had become familiar with the 'River' class frigates and the similar 'Loch' and 'Bay' classes. Most of those built were diesel engined but just six were driven by steam turbines. On 1st April 1949, Townsend purchased the 'River' class frigate *Halladale* from the Admiralty for £15,000. Being a turbine she was vibration free and was therefore ideal for passenger work although her name could not have had further leanings from the English Channel being a river that flows into the north coast of Scotland near Thurso.

The *Halladale* (K417) was built by A&J Inglis at Pointhouse, Glasgow, during 1944 and was launched into the Clyde on 28th January that year. She appears to have served just one commission before she was disposed of in 1949 having been built as an anti-submarine frigate for convoy escort in the North Atlantic to the design of William Reed. Such ships were cheap and quick to build in civilian dockyards. The acquisition was something of a gamble as the Navy did not allow a proper inspection prior to purchase but fortunately dry-docking showed her hull to be in sound condition, although being built for speed, her plates were thin.

Norman Dewar again prepared the conversion plans and the *Halladale* was towed from Portsmouth to the Rushbrooke yard of the Cork Dockyard Co. who quoted a fixed price of £77,000 for the work.

Townsend's new ship was altogether more substantial than the old *Forde*. Her length overall was 301 ft 6 in. and her extreme beam measured 36 ft 6 in. Gross tonnage was 1,370 and four Parsons steam turbines drove her at 20 knots through single reduction gearing. Garage space was for 55 cars and her passenger certificate was for 355 – a huge improvement on the *Forde* but still some way smaller than her competitors at Dover. She was able to complete the crossing between Dover and Calais in a little over the hour and completed her successful maiden voyage on 6th April 1950. At the inaugural lunch on board on the previous day, Townsend stated that the *Halladale* represented the fulfilment of a ten-year ambition for the company. Although it was still believed that the proper way to load cars onto such a vessel was by driving them aboard, during the previous year, despite their passengers' fears, only nine cars had been damaged out of the 11,000 shipped.

On the completion of her first season, the *Halladale* retired to Immingham for refit and continued to visit the Lincolnshire port until after being caught there by an industrial dispute some years later, subsequent refits took place in Amsterdam. During her first overhaul, the ship's appearance was changed somewhat by raising the line of her black hull paint while a new passenger promenade deck was added forward of the bridge thus extending the area of outside deck space.

In 1949 Townsend had purchased a disused 110 ft Callender-Hamilton military bridge from Buroughbridge in Yorkshire. The structure cost the company £2,700 and the intention was to move it to Calais for use as the port's first car ferry linkspan. The bridge was finally adapted for use at the port's berth 3 and was first used by the *Halladale* on 27th June 1951 when, to commemorate the occasion, an eight-ton East Kent coach drove ashore. Four days later the new ramp came into regular use making the *Halladale* the first roll on–roll off passenger ship in the English Channel.

The Port of Dover had to wait until 30th June 1953 until the twin berths in the Camber were opened although the *Halladale* had been using berth 1 since April. The Belgian Marine car ferry service (to Ostend) and that operated by British Railways (to Boulogne) now moved across the harbour from the Admiralty Pier to the Eastern Docks at a time when Townsend was celebrating its silver jubilee there.

From approximately 6,000 cars handled at Dover in 1928, traffic had grown to 31,000 by 1938, 40,000 in 1948, 100,000 in 1950 and 200,000 in 1955. By 1975 over a million cars were being shipped –Townsend had certainly started something.

A powerful view of the converted **Halladale** *which took up the Townsend service in 1950. Throughout her career, the diminutive vessel never lost the air of a Royal Navy frigate. (FotoFlite)*

TOWNSEND LOSES CONTROL

In order to finance the conversion of the *Forde* back in 1929, Townsend had floated the company on the London Stock Exchange. Although the £1 shares were eventually to yield £15, the public interest in the share issue was disappointing and in the event, Townsend had to find most of the money himself. The company therefore remained private until for tax reasons it was floated again in 1956.

In July 1956, continued growth in traffic and the necessity for providing for death duties prompted Townsend to go public. Unfortunately, the share issue was issued on the very day that in Egypt Colonel Nasser announced the nationalisation of the Suez Canal; the country was in crisis,

trade on the Stock Exchange slumped and consequently few shares were sold. Townsend's dream was that his shares would be purchased by small business owners in the ranks of the loyal and contented customers who always chose to cross the Channel in the *Halladale*. He envisaged that he would remain in control of the company that he had founded but matters were to turn out in a totally different way.

It so happened that in Coventry, a group of businessmen were at that time combing the Stock Market for a small company with large assets that they could transfer to their own electrical and property interests. Townsend Bros Car Ferries was such a company with assets of £500,000 ready for the time when a new ship would be ordered. Mr George Nott of Monument Securities, Mr Roland Wickenden (his accountant and financial director) and Mr B.W. Stephenson (his stock broker) gained a 51 per cent controlling interest in the company and what became known as George Nott Industries took the helm. At an extraordinary meeting of the shareholders in April 1957, Townsend and his fellow directors were voted off the board and so ended a notable era in the annals of cross-Channel history.

There is often much ill feeling during a takeover and this was no exception. It was not surprising that there was a great deal of resentment by the existing Townsend board when they realised that Nott simply wished to strip them of their assets and not continue with the ferry at all. Fortunately, matters turned out differently but there had been an earlier time when the Townsend board had been involved with talks with British Railways concerning the possibility of Townsend Bros Car Ferries Ltd becoming a railway subsidiary. The offer from BR was in Townsend's eyes derisory but how different things could have been.

All those who knew Stuart Townsend, the city shipowner, considered him to a gentleman of the 'old school'; gentle, polite, courteous and a man who was frequently on board the ship in a purely social capacity, talking to the passengers whose patronage he so valued.

The company that he had founded was very much a family affair and perhaps, above all else, an interest. He wrote, "It is difficult for me to convey the pride I took in this car-ferrying business and the pleasure it gave me. Because it was a small concern, I was able to keep in close touch with every department."

For the officers and crew of the *Halladale*, they all believed that 1957 would be their last. They had weathered the threat of the Southern Railway and later the nationalised British Railways for nearly 30 years but a time when the Townsend family ceased to be in control of their welfare seemed to be too far off to concern themselves with.

There is little doubt that, above all others, it was Townsend who was the real champion of the roll on–roll off concept at Dover. Right from the start he had seen the future of cross-Channel traffic from the perspective of the motorist and recognised that there was both a need and an opportunity to improve matters. It was now left to others to develop and bring his ideas into fruition. However, the Townsend family name was to continue in use for another 30 years until the formation of P&O European Ferries in 1987.

CAPTAIN DAWSON SAVES THE DAY

Captain John E. Dawson was known to everyone as 'Jack'. He had joined the Townsend ship delivery business shortly after the war before briefly leaving to take a shore job. The *Forde*'s Master was Captain Louis Brady but ill health had forced him to retire early in 1947 and he died shortly afterwards. His Chief Officer, John Hume, was duly promoted Master and Townsend approached Jack Dawson to fill the vacant Chief's position. Both Hume and Dawson accompanied the *Halladale* to Cork to oversee her conversion in 1949-50 but after just two seasons, Hume and Townsend parted ways after a disagreement and John Hume joined British Railways. This left Jack Dawson as Townsend's senior officer and he was duly promoted to Master.

It is difficult to state the degree of influence that Captain Dawson was to exert in his dealings with Townsend and later with George Nott and his fellow directors. Suffice to say that he was always held in the highest esteem and remained Senior Master until his retirement in May 1978. In recognition of his outstanding and unflinching service to the company, he was made Fleet Commodore in 1974. He died, aged 99 in 2011.

Jack Dawson remembered an occasion when he was invited to dinner by the three senior members of the new board. They naturally wished to know everything about their new company and Dawson did his utmost to persuade them that rather than strip Townsend of its assets, they were sitting on a potential gold mine and that the ability for money making was enormous. The mouth-watering attraction of duty-free sales and an involvement in the holiday market where travellers would pay well in advance to secure a booking proved to be decisive. The board obviously liked what they heard and Townsend Bros Car Ferries survived.

The difference between Stuart Townsend and George Nott was chalk and cheese. Townsend's background was that of a wealthy Edwardian businessman – Nott, on the other hand, was very much a self-made man who very quickly came to enjoy the position and importance attached to it. The new

Chairman had no knowledge of ships and the sea apart from the annual outings to the Bristol Channel on which he took his Coventry-based board for excursions on the P&A Campbell fleet. He duly purchased Campbell's from the receiver in December 1959; perhaps for sentiment but also to offset accumulated losses against Townsend's own tax bill.

In 1959, George Nott Industries acquired the whole of Townsend's share capital in a full takeover of the company. It was noted that the occasional lorry did cross the Channel but the new board believed that was a large untapped market to capture. Having a fundamentally different business model to Townsend Car Ferries, British Railways weren't interested in this type of traffic as all goods crossed to Dunkirk in the train ferries. However, at Tilbury, Frank Bustard's Transport Ferry Service was operating a successful lorry service to Antwerp and Townsend aimed to tap into the market.

A RO-RO SHIP

The company now illustrated their forward-looking views by taking on long-term charter from the Ministry of Transport, the twin-screw tank landing ship *Empire Shearwater* (4,285 gross tons) which had been built at Sunderland in 1945. The vessel was one of a large number of similar craft laid up in the Gareloch and idle since the 1956 Suez Crisis. At Tilbury the Transport Ferry Service of the Atlantic Steam Navigation Co. operated a small fleet of similar ships and the charter of the 'Shearwater' offered a cut-rate alternative to the longer overnight North Sea passage. A subsidiary company, European Ferries Ltd, was duly formed to operate the chartered ship and a special linkspan was constructed at the foot of the Eastern Arm inside the Camber. Although her thrice-weekly crossing times could take up to two and a half hours, the bow-loading ship could carry lorries of up to 60 tons in weight with a headroom of 12 ft 6 in.

Amid much optimism, the port's first ever freight service commenced on 10th January 1959. American army lorries and the antiques trade made use of the new service but the Calais customs proved to be over-officious causing delays and ill feeling amongst the shippers. The service closed in June and by the end of September, the ship was laid up in the Medway. It was a brave attempt but in the case of Dover, a few years ahead of its time.

By the late 1950s, the *Halladale* was capacity constrained and unable to cope with all the car ferry traffic on offer. Belgian Marine had introduced a second car ferry on the Ostend route and British Railways had increased capacity on the Boulogne link with the entry into service of the *Lord Warden* (1952) and *Maid of Kent* (1959). French National Railways (SNCF) had introduced their first car ferry in 1958. The *Compiegne* proved to be a very fine and versatile ship and provided stiff competition with the diminutive *Halladale* on the Calais link although it should be noted that, at this time, both ships were still used on a seasonal basis for tourist traffic.

During the *Halladale*'s annual refits at Verschure in Amsterdam, Townsend directors had met and come to an understanding with representatives of their associates NV Werf Gusto of Schiedam concerning a projected new ship. Townsend's naval architect Norman Dewar had died and Burness Corlett was engaged to act on the company's behalf. Unfortunately, George Nott failed to hit if off with their Carew Robinson and so a young, and at that time inexperienced, naval architect on Dewar's staff, James Ayres, was given the responsibility of designing the new ship. Provisional plans for a new twin funnels aft ferry had been drawn up prior to the takeover but in Jimmy Ayres they had employed a man with his own individual ideas and so the designs for the £1 million *Free Enterprise* were born.

In the final year of the *Halladale* (1961), 27,487 cars and 86,744 passengers were carried. She ended her career with Townsend on 5th November and was sold in January the following year to W. Rostedt of Turku, Finland, for £42,000. With passenger capacity raised to 700 and car spaces reduced to ten, she was renamed *Norden* for a ferry service across the Gulf of Bothnia linking Turku and the Swedish port of Norrtalje but was quickly sold again to other Scandinavian owners in June and renamed *Turist Expressen* for service between Turku and Stockholm. In November she was sold a third time, this time to Ferryboats Margarita of Porlamar, Venezuela for a service across the mouth of Lake Maracaibo. There she became the *Ferrymar III* and after 11 more years was eventually laid aside as a hulk before scrapping at Aruba in the West Indies during 1987.

FREE ENTERPRISE

With the building of the *Free Enterprise*, Townsend produced a ferry that was like no other in the English Channel and which proved to be the first multi-purpose vessel capable of carrying passengers, cars and freight. She was unusually broad in the beam compared with her length and her flared bow and pyramidal superstructure gave her something of a yacht-like appearance. She was a revolutionary little ship with an extremely high 15 ft tall stern door ready to cope with the lorry traffic which the Townsend board had anticipated back in 1959 with the *Empire Shearwater*. Her twin funnels led the engine exhausts away from the centre line of the ship and allowed ample head height for traffic on her main vehicle deck without creating a central island around which the traffic would have to flow. The central part of the main vehicle deck was in fact recessed along the centre between the two widely spaced main engines and a hinged ramp could be lowered to take cars up onto the upper Shelter Deck which was an innovation and eventually seen in all eight 'Free Enterprises'. Outside the central vehicle deck area were side alleyways for cars and caravans.

The ship was driven by two 12-cylinder MAN engines and KaMeWa controllable-pitch propellers which greatly assisted manoeuvring in port. Although she was a stern loader, a large 22 ft diameter turntable allowed vehicles to be swung in readiness for driving off in Dover or Calais. Her interior was rather spartan and of open plan design with ship's offices and selling points sited around the perimeter in order to maximise the spending potential of the passengers seated within. This was quite unlike that experienced in the rival railway steamers whose seating areas were generally laid out like confined railway carriages – long and narrow with a corridor between. Although the open plan proved popular and was continued, there was nowhere to escape if a noisy coach party happened to be on board, a problem which was later exaggerated when the four-hour crossing to Zeebrugge was introduced. Yet to the casual observer, the most noticeable feature of the new ship was her livery.

Prior to her entry into service, all cross-Channel ships were painted with black hulls and yet the *Free Enterprise* was

Top: The **Halladale**'s *restaurant seated just 34 people. (A.D. Townsend)*

Above: Captain 'Jack' Dawson welcomes the very first passengers on board the new ***Free Enterprise*** in April 1962. (Ferry Publications Library)

*The **Free Enterprise** during her first 1962 season when her name was painted white on her '**Caronia**' green hull. At the time of publication, the much altered vessel is long laid up near Piraeus. (FotoFlite)*

shockingly pale green. George Nott had taken a fancy to Cunard's 'Green Goddess', the *Caronia,* which he had seen from the bridge of the *Halladale* during a crossing with Captain Dawson, and had decided that his new ship should look the same. He later telephoned Cunard to ask from where they sourced the paint.

The keel of the *Free Enterprise* was laid on 7th August 1961 and she was launched by Mrs Bernice Nott on the following 2nd February – an amazing time of just six months. She was due in service on 12th April but was subject to delays at Schiedam and did not operate her maiden voyage until 22nd April. The new ship could accommodate 850 passengers and 120 cars and in her first full year transported as many as 83,545 cars and 250,000 passengers – well in excess of double the loadings carried by her predecessor in her final season.

The confidence created by the new ship's success was quite staggering. Within her 18-year career, Townsend and 'Free Enterprise' became the English Channel's premier operator and as traffic spiralled, so the basic design of the cross-Channel ferry evolved in order to meet the future challenge. Starved of investment due to concerns about a future Channel Tunnel, the railway fleet struggled valiantly but failed to compete and by 1974, no fewer than eight 'Free Enterprise' ships had taken to the Dover Strait.

One of the reasons why the nationalised British Rail fleet was always hampered was that the period between ordering a new ship and her delivery was always prolonged and required the attention of numerous committees. Townsend's great advantage was that they were able to order ships at the end of one season for delivery at the start of the next. To achieve this aim, it was necessary to have a 'standard' ferry design which could be modified if necessary to suit the changing demands of the industry and forecast traffic growth.

The Townsend board sent James Ayres to Scandinavia to examine the latest examples of ferry design as they were anxious to introduce a drive-through ship of the type which Thoresen Car Ferries had recently established on the ferry routes from Southampton. The result of this visit was the *Free Enterprise II* which at 4,122 gross tons not only became the largest car ferry in service but also the first UK registered drive-through cross-Channel ferry. George Nott's original intention was to have the new ship built on the Clyde by Alexander Stephen & Sons but the yard proved to be extremely slow in confirming that they actually wanted to build the ship and so the job went back to Holland.

The commercial vehicle traffic which had been anticipated at the entry into service of the *Free Enterprise I* (as she had been renamed early in 1965) had failed to materialise and thus the 'FE II' was built with a lower main vehicle deck height of 11ft 2 in. which within a year was to prove her Achilles' heel. Thus the new ship proved to be the least successful of the 'Free Enterprise' series and she was offered for sale within four years of entering service. In spite of her shortcomings, she proved to be an excellent addition for shipping cars and caravans.

The £1.3 million *Free Enterprise II* was launched at Schiedam on 29th January 1965 and entered service on 22nd May. Captain David Bruce joined Townsend from British Rail and thus the ship was the only one of the eight 'Free Enterprises' not to be commanded by Captain Dawson. On the occasion of the ship's press voyage, three days prior to entering service, the 'FE II' had officially opened the second ro-ro berth at Calais, adjacent to the original structure which was still being used by the 'FE I' and the French ferry *Compiegne*. The same occasion saw George Nott made a Freeman of Calais although his influence abruptly stopped following his imprisonment on a drink/ drive charge in 1966 after which the energetic and vigorous Roland Wickenden firmly took the helm of the growing company until his untimely death in October 1972. The company headquarters were immediately moved to Dover and the Midlands-based engineering concerns were gradually disposed of. Roland Wickenden was very much the driving force of the new

*Top: The main vehicle deck of the **Free Enterprise** showing the side galleries and the hanging ramp leading to the Shelter Deck, above. (Ferry Publications Library)*

*Above: The launch of the **Free Enterprise II** at Schiedam in January 1965. (Ferry Publications Library)*

Townsend and being unpretentious, articulate and highly intelligent, greatly impressed all those that knew him. Under Wickenden's leadership, and later that of his brother Keith, Townsend Car Ferries undoubtedly saw its finest days.

ZEEBRUGGE

The first great change to the established pattern of Channel services occurred on 17th March 1966 when the *Free Enterprise II* inaugurated a new service linking Dover with the Belgian port of Zeebrugge. The crossing time was four hours with the ship regularly leaving Dover at midday and berthing in the entrance to the canal that led to Bruges. Here the vehicles were offloaded via a floating pontoon called *Auto-Carrier* which was moved out of the way when the ship left port. A two hour thirty minute turn round was allowed and the vessel was back in Dover at 22.30. Although the 'FE II' was incapable of carrying high-sided vehicles, she led the way for the £2 million *Free Enterprise III* which went down the ways at Schiedam on 14th May 1966 and arrived in Dover for trials, at the newly opened double-deck berth 4, on 21st July. After carrying out her maiden voyage to Calais on the following day, she was transferred to the Zeebrugge link on the following 15th January bringing a 20 per cent increase in freight capacity on the route.

The 'FE III' was very much a transitional vessel and had she been built 18 months later then she would have certainly been a totally different ship. She was built to carry either 221 cars or 14 pieces of freight (in her wing decks) with 102 cars. With freight demanding ever more space and the size and weight of lorries increasing, the crews struggled to load her frequently using wooden wedges and soapy water to slide the heavy wheels into position in the freight alleys. It was the 'FE III' that established Zeebrugge as the company's principal freight port. During 1966 just 2,687 pieces of freight were shipped by the three Townsend ferries while 1967 saw this traffic leap to 17,250 – an increase of 600 per cent – three quarters of which was carried on the Zeebrugge link.

*Right: A splendid view of the **Free Enterprise II** when new and flying the Townsend Bros Car Ferries house flag (three ships within a white diamond) from her mainmast. She was the first British registered drive-through ferry. (FotoFlite)*

*The Townsend fleet at Dover in 1966 with (left to right) the **Free Enterprise II**, **Free Enterprise I** and **Free Enterprise III** at the lay-by berth in the Camber. (Ferry Publications Library)*

HOVERCRAFT, FREIGHT SHIPS AND THORESEN ASSISTS

The year 1966 also saw Townsend experiment with a Westland SRN6 passenger-carrying hovercraft. The 38-seater vessel, named *Britannia*, commenced operations on 30th April operating under the wing of the Townsend subsidiary P&A Campbell Ltd. Sadly, the venture was not a success and with weather and technical problems causing operational difficulties, the final crossing to Calais was made on 30th September. The craft appeared again in 1967 running off the beach excursions from Leysdown, Margate, Folkestone, Greatstone and Hastings before eventually being returned to its owners.

At the end of 1966, the long-established General Steam Navigation Company (GSNC) withdrew their three coastal excursion ships and ceased trading as Eagle Steamers. One of these vessels was the *Royal Sovereign* which had been built in 1948 by the famous Dumbarton shipbuilders, William Denny & Bros. The ship was laid up in Deptford Creek and Townsend

eventually purchased her for £100,000, promptly sending her to Amsterdam for a total rebuild costing a further £150,000.

The result was the roll on–roll off freight ship *Autocarrier* which could carry 24 pieces of freight and 36 drivers. The initial plan was to raise the passenger numbers to between 400 and 500 thereby allowing the ship to run pier-hopping excursions by day under the banner of P&A Campbell Ltd, and freight to Zeebrugge by night. The excursions were being advertised as late as April 1967 for commencement in June mainly sailing from Thanet or Deal piers to Clacton, Southend or simply cruising in the Channel. In addition, there were eight Sundays when trips from Hastings to the Isle of Wight were offered but sadly all of this came to nothing as so much freight was on offer at Zeebrugge that this demanded double daily crossings.

The ship duly arrived at Dover on 27th August 1967 and undertook her maiden crossing three days later. Unfortunately, on her return to Dover she developed engine problems which saw only 9 of her 24 engine cylinders firing thus slowing her to a 9 hour 30 minute crossing time. With a single skin hull and being lightly built for the summer tourist trade, the ship was not ideally suited for year round freight operation and proved to be a particularly wet vessel which earned her the nickname of 'Townsend's submarine'.

During October 1967, the *Autocarrier* was extensively damaged while running astern into the canal at Zeebrugge and she was out of service for six months. A hastily arranged charter of SNCF's *Chantilly* took place before the Thoresen freighter *Viking IV* appeared to fill the gap. Then in late December came the Swedish ferry *Stena Danica* which commenced a lengthy charter, continuing after the *Autocarrier*'s return in the following May. The *Autocarrier* remained in service until sold to Italian interests in October 1973 when she was renamed *Ischia*. With her passenger accommodation restored two years later, she remained in service between Naples and Ischia until 2007 by which time she was almost 60. Although her time with Townsend was relatively brief, she helped to establish the Zeebrugge link and the company's reputation as the premier freight shipper to Belgium.

An unfortunate mishap on the *Free Enterprise III* occurred during November 1968 when a road tanker spilled liquid nitrogen onto her vehicle deck resulting in considerable damage to the deck and cross-beams. She immediately returned to the Belgian port discharging her vehicles at the train ferry berth before retiring for repairs during which time a Quiet Lounge was added between the funnel and the bridge. It did nothing for the ship's overall appearance but was certainly required, especially on the overnight service to Belgium.

The 'FE I' was immediately switched to the four-hour link for three days before the Thoresen ferry *Viking II* was brought up the Channel from Southampton to cover. Townsend had acquired Thoresen in September that year thereby creating the European Ferries Group and this was the first example of inter-fleet co-operation within the joint company. Sister ship *Viking I* also appeared on the Zeebrugge link from December 1969 until January 1970.

MORE 'FREE ENTERPRISES' JOIN THE FLEET

Until Townsend opened their service to Zeebrugge in 1966, the historic Belgian Marine link to nearby Ostend was the

Top: The **Free Enterprise V** *is seen shortly after her launch at Schiedam in January 1970. (Ferry Publications Library)*

Above: The freight ship **Autocarrier** *was converted from the General Steam Navigation Co's excursion vessel* **Royal Sovereign**. *(FotoFlite)*

Top: The **Free Enterprise IV** *loading for Zeebrugge at Dover's new berth 4. (John Hendy)*

Above: The **Free Enterprise VII** *nears her home port at the close of her delivery voyage in February 1973. (FotoFlite)*

principal UK-Belgium corridor. The state-owned shipping line operated a fleet of seven passenger vessels (including one built that year) and four car ferries. All were very fast and traditional-looking ships with long, lean lines but their car ferry fleet failed to adapt to the changing traffic trends and was soon being outstripped by their British-based rivals. Townsend had experienced a great degree of hostility from the Belgian Government over the construction of a purpose-built terminal at Zeebrugge and, as carriers of 80 per cent of the UK-Belgian traffic at that time, were reluctant to allow Townsend's ambitious plans to take place. Roland Wickenden announced that the decision to build a fourth 'Free Enterprise' very much depended on a change of attitude from the Belgian Government.

The *Free Enterprise IV* was launched on 1st March 1969 and was delivered on 28th May – an amazingly short period. After trials on the following day she was in service to Zeebrugge on 1st June. Jimmy Ayres' design was deemed to be so successful that the rest of the 'Free Enterprise' series followed and developed the basic plan – here at last was the pattern for future tonnage and on which Townsend would build their success. The 'FE IV' was the ship that established Townsend and Zeebrugge as a major player in the cross-Channel arena. With capacity for 260 cars or 24 pieces of freight, the ship was also the first to employ the triple screw/ single rudder arrangement which her four sisters duly followed. Experience soon showed that when the centre screw was not being used, it tended to hide the rudder thereby reducing the effectiveness of the two remaining propellers. This was remedied in the remaining ships of the class. Unlike the first three 'Enterprises', her vehicle decks had short casings and as the centre lanes were not lowered, the extra space allowed lorries to manoeuvre more easily.

On 1st April 1972, the 'FE IV' officially opened the new Zeebrugge car ferry terminal at the shore end of the port's famous mole. Such was the ship's success and the flourishing new service to Belgium that the rest of the 'Free Enterprise' series were in turn allocated to the route while the older units were employed on the Calais link. On the arrival of the 'FE IV' into service, the *Free Enterprise II* was offered for sale but in the event was mainly used for seasonal tourist sailings on which she was particularly successful.

The £2.5 million *Free Enterprise V* was launched at Schiedam on 31st January 1970 and arrived at Dover on 23rd May. Four days later she undertook a special sailing to Zeebrugge with army personnel and returned full of freight. The maiden commercial voyage took place on 31st May.

During December 1970, Townsend Thoresen announced a five-ship building programme, two of which were destined for Dover; the 'FE VI' in April 1972 and the 'FE VII' in the following February. Although looking very similar to the previous vessels in the series, in a major development of the class they were given three important modifications. The interior platform decks allowed them to carry 314 cars as opposed to the 260 of the earlier ships while mechanically they were fitted with the more powerful Stork-Werkspoor engines rather than the Smit-MAN engines used previously. A third modification was that they were given fin stabilisers in place of the earlier passive flume-stabilisers which had proved far less successful than had been anticipated.

The *Free Enterprise VI* was launched at Schiedam on 29th January 1972 but although she was scheduled to her maiden voyage to Zeebrugge on 15th June, did not arrive in Dover until late on the following day. She was promptly returned to the builders with a fault in her exhaust system concerning the bellows which kept cracking and leaking gases. Being a ship short, the company were forced to charter the diminutive Sealink (British Rail) turbine steamer *Normannia* for the Calais service until 26th June.

On her return to Dover on 28th June, the 'FE VI' carried out the usual trials and crew familiarisation period before entering service some two days later. From 8th July, her schedules were changed and two daylight services to Calais were inserted between on overnight run to Zeebrugge. During the summers of 1973 and 1974, without the slots available at Calais for extra weekend sailings, Townsend turned to Boulogne when an extra 30 sailings were added to the timetable.

The *Free Enterprise VII*'s career was to closely mirror that of her immediate predecessor although there was an obvious exterior difference when for navigational reasons, her mainmast was sited further astern and not on the roof of the

Top: The **Free Enterprise IV** *speeds away from Dover to Boulogne late in her career. (FotoFlite)*

Above: The **Free Enterprise III** *leaves Dover Western Docks during a brief charter to Sealink UK Ltd in July 1981. (A.G. Jones)*

after deckhouse. A further modification took place when she was given inward turning propellers which proved to be so successful that all subsequent ferries were similarly treated. Both the centre and port screws were right turning while the starboard propeller was left turning. This produced a paddle wheel effect which greatly improved their handling characteristics.

The 'FE VII' was launched on 21st October 1972 but the occasion was tinged with sadness when Roland Wickenden died on the train back to Zeebrugge during his return to England. The ship was delivered on 23rd February 1973 and carried out her maiden voyage to Zeebrugge three days later.

The final ship of the 'Free Enterprise' series was the *Free Enterprise VIII* which was six metres longer than the earlier ships and built at the Verolme Shipyard at Alblasserdam rather than Schiedam. She was the only one of the eight Townsend ships not to appear in the pale green hull colours so favoured by George Nott back in the early sixties as the white letters of the company's 'Townsend Thoresen' name failed to make the required impression. A darker green was therefore introduced for two years until Thoresen orange hulls were adopted as the standard fleet livery in 1976.

Senior Master, Captain Jack Dawson, persuaded the local management that the ship would be too long for Calais and she was therefore mainly associated with the Zeebrugge link. Captain Dawson later admitted to the writer that the longer route to Belgium was always his preference and therefore made a special case that his final command should exclusively work that route. Of the eight 'Free Enterprise' class vessels, the 'FE VIII' was the only one to remain operating from her port of registry throughout the period of her UK service. The ship was launched on 6th April 1974 and worked her maiden voyage to Zeebrugge on 18th July. With the Dover fleet only requiring seven vessels with which to work the Calais and Zeebrugge rosters, the 'FE III' was switched to the company's new North Channel service across the Irish Sea.

Between 1974 and 1979, all eight 'Free Enterprise' class

*Right: The **Free Enterprise V** is seen in her period of service in the Western Channel during 1982-85. (FotoFlite)*

*The longer **Free Enterprise VIII** was the last of the 'FE' series and was built at Alblasserdam in 1974. (FotoFlite)*

ferries were in operation together. The 'FE I' was tried on the Cairnryan-Larne route during 1975 while the 'FE IV' was moved to the North Channel for the 1976 season. She, in turn, proved to be so successful that she remained on station for a further ten years as the older units of the fleet began to spend winter periods at lay-up. By 1976 the 'FE I' was laid up all summer at Calais and was only used at peak periods. She finished with her final crossing on the Dover-Calais route on Christmas Eve 1979. It was then to Tilbury for lay-up before her departure to Greece as the *Kimolos* in February 1980. She had served the company for 18 years by which time the success of Townsend had completely and utterly overtaken her. Loved by all, she was simply too small for the volume of traffic now on offer and with a completely new class of ferry then under construction in Germany she was totally eclipsed. Thirty-two years later, the much-altered former *Free*

Enterprise is still afloat although not likely to operate again. Her half a century of service is remarkable.

DOUBLE-DECKED FREIGHT SHIPS

Following the departure of the *Autocarrier* to Italian interests in 1973, the new *Stena Sailer* was also taken on charter. Townsend then chartered the ro-ro vessel *Scandinavia* to ship extra freight to Zeebrugge in the 1974 season. The Swedish ship was owned by R/A Nordo of Malmo and completed her service during mid-December.

The continuing demand for freight saw the group's Technical Director James Ayres visiting European shipyards for a standard design roll on-roll off ship which could be adapted for Townsend Thoresen's use. Schichau Unterweser AG (SUAG) of Bremerhaven duly built three identical sisters capable of carrying 46 freight units, 32 export cars, 52 cabin berths for lorry drivers and passenger certificates for 132. They were the first local double-decked freight vessels and proved to be a tremendous advance on anything else previously seen. The first of the trio was the *European Gateway* for the Felixstowe station; she was followed by the *European Trader* which was launched on 30th May 1975 and entered service on 18th October using the new double-deck ramp at Camber B which had been constructed adjacent to berth 1. The *European Clearway* completed the three-ship order and having been launched on 10th October 1975, after a spell on the Felixstowe-Europort link, duly entered service from Dover to Zeebrugge on 15th February 1976.

Following the huge success of the original trio of ships, a fourth was ordered to the company's full specification and which included a number of modifications deemed necessary after operational experience with the earlier vessels. The most obvious change was in the fitting of fin stabilisers that proved far more effective than the passive versions in the other ships. The *European Enterprise* was launched in December 1977 and entered service at Dover on the following 29th April.

COMPETITION BRINGS A REVOLUTIONARY TRIO

What turned out to be the final decade of Townsend Thoresen began with the promise of the most intensive cross-Channel war in the history of the Dover Strait services.

Throughout the 1950s and 1960s, British Railways (later Sealink UK Ltd) had concentrated their car ferry services on the Dover-Boulogne link but from 1970 onwards had moved the entire thrust of their operation to Calais in competition with the Townsend service. In this, they were assisted by SNCF, their state-owned French partners. Promised for the summer of 1980 were two new multi-purpose vehicle ferries from Harland & Wolff's Belfast yard while the French were planning a third such vessel to be built in Le Havre. The three ferries were to be larger than any others then in service and boasted twin freight decks enabling simultaneous two-deck loading/ unloading on both sides of the Dover Strait. New berths (numbers 5 and 6) would be built to accommodate the ships and Dover Harbour Board reclaimed a further six acres of seabed in order to provide sufficient standage areas. At Calais, an entirely new port was constructed to the seaward

*The **European Clearway** was the third of a quartet of freight ships built at Bremerhaven and entered service to Zeebrugge in October 1975. (FotoFlite)*

end of the Gare Maritime.

The order for the Sealink ferries was placed in May 1979 and, somewhat caught out by this surprise move, Townsend Thoresen responded almost immediately to this unwelcome intervention. Their contribution to the uprated services was the 'Spirit' class trio which, although unconventional in appearance, were technically very advanced and allowed the company to run five daily round trips to Calais at speeds of 24 knots which the short-sea routes had not seen for many years. Although these eventually settled down to 75-minute crossings, the writer crossed in under an hour during his first sailing in the *Spirit of Free Enterprise* just five days after she had entered service.

In an attempt to reduce the ships' centre of gravity, James Ayres unusually narrowed their superstructure and recessed the lifeboats either side of the upper vehicle deck. The distance to the water was certainly reduced although the design was unusual and modernist. The amount of outside deck space allocated to passengers was also a disappointment for many who had come to expect the wide spaces provided by the earlier ships of the fleet.

What turned out to be the ships' most controversial innovation was the use of slide around 'Neat-Stow' bow (and stern) doors which replaced the normal 'up and over' bow visors. The visor was perhaps the most vulnerable part of earlier drive-through car ferry design but the 'Neat-Stow' doors were tucked inside the ships' belting and therefore the risk of damage when berthing was greatly decreased.

Townsend Thoresen went back to SUAG at Bremerhaven for their three new ships which all eventually appeared months before the British Rail (Sealink) twins which suffered endless delays at Belfast.

The *Spirit of Free Enterprise* was launched sideways on 21st July 1979 and eventually operated her maiden voyage from Dover to Calais on 14th January 1980. The arrival of the new ships saw off the earlier generation ferries. April and May

*Left: The **Spirit of Free Enterprise** was the lead ship of a controversial trio of ro-ro passenger ships which enabled five round crossings to Calais to be operated each day. She was later renamed **Pride of Kent** and stretched at Palermo. (FotoFlite)*

*P&O Normandy Ferries' **nf Tiger** joined her sister **nf Panther** and the earlier **Lion** on the Dover-Boulogne route in June 1978. (FotoFlite)*

1980 saw the 'FE II' back on the Calais link for the final time before finishing service between Portsmouth and Cherbourg that summer. The 'FE III' meanwhile operated this seasonal service in 1981 while the 'FE V' also found her way into the Western Channel.

The fast crossings of the 'Spirit' enabled Townsend Thoresen to market Dover-Calais as 'The Blue Riband Route' and she clocked 53 minutes 49 seconds pier-to-pier which was certainly a vehicle ferry record and eventually bettered by her sister ships.

The *Herald of Free Enterprise* was launched at SUAG on 21st December 1979 before entering service at Dover on 29th May the following year. On 10th July she crossed to Calais in a Force 8 gale in a pier-to-pier time of 52 minutes 53 seconds at an average speed of 24.73 knots. The trio was complete with

the arrival of the *Pride of Free Enterprise* which replaced the 'FE III' in the fleet and which carried out her maiden voyage on 23rd November 1980 having been launched at Bremerhaven on 31st May. She broke her sister's crossing record by just four seconds on 9th February 1982.

P&O NORMANDY FERRIES

As has previously been seen, until 1970 British Rail (later Sealink UK Ltd) had operated vehicle ferries on the Dover-Boulogne route but after that year, the service was gradually downgraded as more sailings were directed at Calais. Seeing an opportunity of filling the void and finding themselves with a spare ferry, P&O Normandy Ferries transferred their ship *Lion* to Dover and she commenced service in April 1976. The ship had been built for the Ardrossan-Belfast route of the P&O

subsidiary Burns & Laird but the political 'troubles' in the Province had badly affected loadings and the service had been suspended. The nine-year-old ferry was soon joined by the former internal Danish ferry *nf Tiger* (ex *Kattegat*), which entered service at Dover in June 1978 and then by her sister *nf Panther* (ex *Djursland*) in January 1980.

The service was fairly basic and the three ferries were small so that it was difficult to make any large scale on-board improvements. For a while they thrived at Sealink's expense but the introduction of new and larger ferries on the Calais link simply served to highlight their shortcomings. There was no money available to build replacements and on 4th January 1985 came the news that the whole operation (including that at Southampton) had been purchased by Townsend Thoresen for £12.5 million.

At the time of the purchase, the *Lion* was serving at Southampton and so did not return to Dover. Of the other two ships, great efforts were made to bring their interiors up to Townsend's standards but the service had been losing money for some time and so Townsend acted by bringing back the *Free Enterprise IV* (from Cairnryan-Larne) and the *Free Enterprise V* (from Portsmouth-Cherbourg) in order to improve matters.

The 'FE V' had been a Portsmouth ship ever since 1982 although had returned to her port of registry on a number of occasions. However, she replaced the *nf Tiger* on 18th July 1986 while the 'FE IV' returned to Dover on 13th July 1986. Following a thorough refit, she duly returned to service on 3rd August replacing the *nf Panther* which joined her sister at Chatham for lay-up.

STRETCHING FOR ZEEBRUGGE

With even more freight space required on the Zeebrugge link, the company decided to invest some £45 million on rebuilding the *Free Enterprise VI* and *Free Enterprise VII* (in addition to two Portsmouth Super-Vikings). The Dover twins were sent to SUAG at Bremerhaven with the 'FE VI' arriving there in June 1985 and the 'FE VII' departing immediately on her return in early November.

After cutting, four mammoth cranes were used to lift the superstructures, each weighing 1,260 tons, which were then

*Cranes lift the superstructure of the **Free Enterprise VI** from her hull section during her rebuilding at Bremerhaven in June 1985. (Ferry Publications Library)*

deposited on the quaysides to await their new forward hull sections. The keel for the 135 metre long forebodies had been laid in January 1985 and launched on 18th May after which it was cut in two and welded back onto the after end of the original hulls. Once this was accomplished, the superstructures were lifted and placed back on their new hull sections. This was an amazing piece of engineering which demanded inch perfect precision throughout. Now capable of accommodating 60 lorries (instead of the previous 24) the 'FE VI' restarted service on 28th October while the 'FE VII' recommenced on the following 9th March.

The results of this intricate ship surgery were certainly not pretty to look at but served to solve an immediate problem which saved the expense and delay of building new ships. The accommodation sections remained the same but the hulls were extended forward and given a completely new upper freight deck.

During the absence of the two Zeebrugge ships, the *Free Enterprise V* was brought back from Portsmouth to cover while the elderly former Atlantic Steam Navigation Co's *Gaelic Ferry* assisted with freight between July and December.

*Top: RMT, the Belgian State operators of the Ostend-Dover service, became Townsend Thoresen's operating partners in 1986. Here is their **Prinses Maria-Esmeralda** approaching her home port. (Mike Louagie)*

*Above: The **Herald of Free Enterprise** was the second of the 1980 trio of ships for the Calais service. Her tragic loss off Zeebrugge in February 1987 brought about the demise of the Townsend Thoresen name. (Miles Cowsill)*

THE 'CHUNNEL BEATERS' AND FLEET EXPANSION

Following the announcement in July 1985 that the British and French Governments were to construct a railway tunnel beneath the Dover Strait, Townsend Thoresen announced their own plans for what they termed, the 'Chunnel Beaters'. These were two giant vessels which they claimed would threaten the financial viability of the tunnel. As with all classes of ferries designed by James Ayres, the new ships were to be a development of the previous trio and after a staff competition to choose names, *Pride of Dover* and *Pride of Calais* were selected. At 26,443 gross tons, the new ships could each carry 2,260 passengers, 650 cars or 100 x 15-metre freight units and by far exceeded the dimensions and capacity of the rest of the fleet. The first went down the ways at SUAG's Bremen yard on 20th September 1986 having been launched by the wife of Mr Geoffrey Parker who since July that year had been the company's Managing Director following the resignation of Mr Kenneth Siddle. Using the most up-to-date methods of prefabricated ship construction, the new ferry quickly took shape, although neither she nor her sister would enter service for the company for which they were built.

Ever since 1846, the historic link between Ostend and Dover had been operated by the Belgian Marine Administration although it was not until 1862 that the Government-owned shipping company had gained a monopoly on the route. This state of affairs continued until March 1966 when, in spite of strong representations from neighbouring Ostend, Townsend had opened their rival Dover-Zeebrugge service. More protests were forthcoming after Townsend had sought to construct a new £300,000 terminal at the foot of the mole when pressure was brought to bear on the Belgian Minister of Transport to thwart the move.

In 1972, Regie Voor Maritiem Transport (or RMT as Belgian Marine had become) had allowed British trading partners Sealink UK Ltd a 15 per cent share of their Ostend traffic when in July, twin overnight sailings from Folkestone were commenced. The partnership continued amicably until Sealink UK was denationalised in July 1984. As part of a general reappraisal of routes by new owners, the Bermuda-based Sea Containers, they made it known that it was their intention to

*The stretched **Free Enterprise VII** sails across a glass-like English Channel. Her sister did not show the TT logo on her after superstructure. (FotoFlite)*

capture a 50 per cent slice in the market and duly switched their ferry *St David* from the Irish Sea.

This aggressive and clumsy move was certainly not to RMT's liking and they duly responded to this gesture by entering into negotiations with their former rivals. These were completed by October 1985 and from New Year's Day 1986 a new five-year agreement came into force which basically gave Townsend Thoresen a 63 per cent slice of all commercial freight carried on the Belgian routes while the same percentage was taken by the Belgians for coaches, their passengers, rail passengers and all other non-accompanied passengers. All other traffic was to be marketed by Townsend Thoresen and the Belgian fleet of ten vessels (seven ro-ro ships, one purely passenger vessel and two Boeing jetfoils)

adopted orange hulls with the Townsend Thoresen trading name while retaining the yellow funnel and logo of RMT.

P&O ACQUIRE THE EUROPEAN FERRIES GROUP

The European Ferries Group (EFG) was not only involved with the UK ferry industry. During the 1970s, the Group began to diversify and acquired Larne Harbour and the Felixstowe Dock & Railway Co. Following this a UK-based property division was formed, its major asset being almost 35 per cent in Stockley plc, a listed property company operating in south east England.

In 1979 the Group became involved with US property with substantial holdings in Denver, Houston and Atlanta. This was followed by further property acquisitions at La Manga Club in

*P&O Normandy Ferries was taken over by the European Ferries Group in 1985 when the **nf Tiger** (foreground) and **nf Panther** were repainted in Townsend Thoresen livery before their replacement in the following year. (FotoFlite)*

Spain and also in West Germany.

However, in January 1986 the P&O Group took a controlling interest in a company holding almost 21 per cent of the EFG shares and at the Board's invitation, they were joined by the P&O Chairman Sir Jeffrey Sterling.

The drop in oil prices was to have a disastrous effect on the EFG's assets in Denver and Houston and financial experts expressed the view that ever since the tragic death of Keith Wickenden in an aeroplane crash at Shoreham during July 1983, the Group had lost its direction. It was stated in the daily press that the Group was in such a financial mess that the directors begged Sir Jeffrey to rescue them and act as their life raft. This duly occurred on 5th December 1986. Trading in

both EFG and P&O shares was suspended on the previous day and EFG shareholders were offered four new P&O shares for every 17 of their own. European Ferries were worth £280 million and reported a £17 million profit in 1985 although strikes cost the company some £10 million and weakened their position.

Whether or not P&O would have eventually totally absorbed the fleet of Townsend Thoresen into their own is not known although it seems likely that some sort of livery change, if not a change of name, was inevitable. However, in March 1987 an event occurred which made it impossible for Townsend Thoresen to continue in name or livery.

DISASTER AT ZEEBRUGGE

On the evening of 6th March 1987, the *Herald of Free Enterprise*, which was deputising on the route, left Zeebrugge with both her outer weatherproof and her inner watertight bow doors wide open.

Within 10 minutes of casting off the ship was passing the end of the new harbour breakwaters, speed was increased to 16 knots and the ship was turned to port. The 'Herald' had been trimmed at the bow in order to allow a proper port fit with the Zeebrugge linkspan. As she increased speed, so she began to scoop up water onto her main vehicle deck causing her to become unstable and leading to her eventual and inevitable capsize. Disaster overtook her so quickly that it had not even been possible to issue a 'Mayday' distress call and had it not been for the shallowness of the water, she would probably have disappeared with all on board. Of the 573 passengers and crew, 193 were lost in Britain's worst ever ferry disaster.

At the public enquiry into the sinking, evidence was given to show that this failure to close the ship's bow doors was not an isolated incident. The company were accused of being too money-minded and had refused to install more powerful trim pumps which would have ensured that the ships would have sailed on an even keel, even although these would have cost a mere £25,000 per ship. Although it was possible to see the open bow doors from the bridge wings, there was no indicator system on the bridge which would alert the Master and his officers if the doors were not closed. The Sheen enquiry revealed a culture of sloppiness throughout Townsend Thoresen's operations.

Images of the stricken 'Herald' lying on her port side with her bow doors gaping wide soon circulated in the world's press and it was crucial that new owners P&O stamped their authority on what was not only a human but also a public relations nightmare. Within days, the rest of the fleet were having their 'TT' funnel logos removed in preparation for repainting in the pale blue with the company flag of P&O Ferries. With the company a ship short, plans were taken in hand to charter the spare Sealink British Ferries multi-purpose ferry *Vortigern* for a period of 60 days commencing on

1st April. She was placed on the Dover-Boulogne service while the 'FE V' was switched to the Calais link until replaced by the new *Pride of Dover* on 2nd June.

As for the 'Herald', she was eventually righted on 7th April and towed into Zeebrugge Harbour. On 5th October, accompanied by the former *Gaelic Ferry*, she was towed away from Flushing (Vlissingen) for scrapping in Taiwan.

Between times, the second 'Chunnel Beater' was launched at Bremen on 11th April and in respect for all those who had died at Zeebrugge, a minute's silence was observed before she took to the water.

The long-awaited arrival of the *Pride of Dover* was, needless to say, a very low-key affair, especially as the Sheen enquiry into the sinking was ongoing. The first of the £46 million 'Chunnel Beaters' was handed over by SUAG on 27th May after a construction period of just 16 months. She was the final ship to enter service (on 2nd June) carrying the Townsend Thoresen banner and with the well-known orange hull.

The year 1987 was certainly the *annus horribilis* of the Dover-based ferry industry. The name of Townsend Thoresen will sadly be linked to one tragic event although it will have been seen that the company and its illustrious predecessor achieved so much during the period of their formation. Just as the events of that night in March 1987 should never be forgotten, so neither should we forget the achievements of Stuart Townsend whose vision and enterprise gave Dover the basis of the industry on which the port was to prosper. Neither should we forget the Wickenden brothers – Roland and Keith – under whose guidance the company developed and a solid foundation for future growth was established so that the company became the leading English Channel ferry operator.

P&O EUROPEAN FERRIES

On 21st October 1987, a new ferry company came into being with the launch of P&O European Ferries. In their press advertisements, the company stressed that their history stretched back to 1837 and indicated that with their experience, passengers would be in good hands. Banished was the bright Thoresen orange livery and in its place, P&O introduced a far more subdued navy blue colour scheme in order to try and regain the public's confidence in the service.

*Top: During her first season in service, the **Pride of Dover** carried the Townsend Thoresen hull livery with a pale blue P&O funnel. During October 1987, P&O European Ferries was created when blue hulls were adopted. (FotoFlite)*

*Above: The freighter **European Clearway** was the first in the local fleet to receive the new livery. Here she arrives at Dover with the stretched **Free Enterprise VI** and **Free Enterprise V** both in port. (FotoFlite)*

Ships were inevitably renamed and the 'Free Enterprise' names were abandoned thus:

Townsend name:	P&O European Ferries name:
Free Enterprise V	*Pride of Hythe*
Free Enterprise VI	*Pride of Sandwich*
Free Enterprise VII	*Pride of Walmer*
Free Enterprise VIII	*Pride of Canterbury*
Spirit of Free Enterprise	*Pride of Kent*
Pride of Free Enterprise	*Pride of Bruges*
European Enterprise	*European Endeavour*

Following the entry into service of the *Pride of Dover*, the *Pride of Calais* ran her maiden commercial voyage on 4th December 1987. The 'FE IV' completed service to Boulogne on that day, destored and was sent to Chatham for disposal while the 'FE VIII' was transferred from the Zeebrugge link to Boulogne in her place. Meanwhile, the *Pride of Free Enterprise* switched from the Calais service to Zeebrugge, her new name *Pride of Bruges* recognising the tremendous debt of gratitude the company owed to the Belgian city for all its support and effort following the disaster of the previous March.

The construction of the Channel Tunnel and the threats that it would bring weighed heavily on the new P&O European Ferries board. At that time, apart from Calais, full passenger services were also operated to Zeebrugge and Boulogne and it was felt that in the longer term, this state of affairs would simply serve to weaken the company's position on the premier Calais link. The opening of the tunnel would act as a magnet to the shortest route and the company aimed at operating their own 'seamless' service to compete with it. Accordingly, it was announced that as from 31st December 1991, the passenger service to Belgium would close with the *Pride of Walmer* operating the final advertised sailing. As from 5th January 1992, the ship was switched to the Calais route to cover for refits before a brief transfer to the Boulogne link. On 5th June she left for a Falmouth refit before taking up operations across the North Channel.

The withdrawal of the passenger service to Zeebrugge was

*Above left: The launch of the **Pride of Dover** at Bremen in September 1986. (Ferry Publications Library)*

*Above: The stretching of the **Pride of Kent** at Palermo (Sicily) in early 1992. (Ferry Publications Library)*

*Left: The first of a projected quartet of super-freighters, the **European Seaway**, is seen immediately after her launch in April 1991. (Ferry Publications Library)*

*The **European Seaway** approaches Dover on her arrival from the builders in October 1991. (FotoFlite)*

not quite as drastic as it might have appeared as P&O's Belgian partners, RMT, continued to operate their service from Ostend to Dover and easily absorbed all the tourist traffic on offer.

As for 'jumboised' sister *Pride of Sandwich*, she completed her final sailing on the Zeebrugge link on 3rd January being replaced by the new freighter *European Pathway*. Then, after a brief spell of service on the Felixstowe-Zeebrugge service she too sailed for a refit at Falmouth before moving to the North Channel in March.

There had been an option to build a third vessel in the *Pride of Dover* series but in the event this was not taken up. Instead,

the company decided that in December 1991 the *Pride of Kent* (ex *Spirit of Free Enterprise*) should be sent to Palermo (Sicily) for refurbishment and stretching by 31.5 metres in order to make her compatible with the 'Dover' and the 'Calais'. The work involved a total rebuild of her accommodation which increased her passenger numbers to 1,850 and her vehicle deck space to 460 cars or 64 x 15-metre commercial vehicles, the work was not deemed to be a total success and it was therefore decided to leave the *Pride of Bruges* (ex *Pride of Free Enterprise*) in her original configuration although much internal improvement was carried out.

The Boulogne route was the next to be axed 'with immediate effect' on 4th January 1993 after which the *Pride of Hythe* and *Pride of Canterbury* (which operated the final service) went to Tilbury to await disposal. With their passing from the fleet, after a period of 31 years, the last of the former 'Free Enterprise' series of ships also disappeared from the Dover Strait.

Between 1991 and 1993, P&O invested £235 million in their Dover operations and the fleet was effectively rebuilt to prepare it for the undoubted challenges which the Channel Tunnel would bring.

NEW FREIGHTERS FOR OLD

The keel for the first of what was originally intended to be a series of four identical freighters was laid at Schichau Seebeckwerft at Bremerhaven on 15th October 1990. At 22,986 gross tons, the 179.7-metre ferry was designed to carry as many as 124 x 15-metre commercial vehicles and up to 200 drivers. The *European Seaway* was duly launched on 20th April the following year and eventually took up service between Dover and Zeebrugge on 7th October 1991. She was followed by the *European Pathway* on 4th January 1992 and then by the

*The second of the twin 'Chunnel Beaters', the **Pride of Calais**, is newly painted in her P&O European Ferries livery. (FotoFlite)*

Top: The **Pride of Walmer** *was originally the* **Free Enterprise VII** *and in 1992 moved to the North Channel as the* **Pride of Rathlin**. *(FotoFlite)*

Below: *The* **Pride of Hythe** *enters Boulogne on an afternoon sailing from Dover. (John Hendy)*

Right: *The newly stretched* **Pride of Kent** *arrives at Dover Eastern Docks in June 1992 and is welcomed by the* **Pride of Hythe**, **Pride of Calais** *and the* **European Pathway**. *(FotoFlite)*

third ship, *European Highway* which took up service on 16th June 1992. The fourth ship was originally intended to be the *European Causeway* but was converted on the stocks to become the *Pride of Burgundy* (28,138 gross tons) for the Dover-Calais service. Following her launch on 16th May 1992, she carried out her maiden voyage on 5th April 1993 joining the company's own five-ship, seamless, 45-minute 'shuttle' service across the Dover Strait a whole year before the tunnel opened for business. In a further move to improve on-board standards and passenger comfort, Club Class lounges were also introduced recreating a First Class excellence which had been missing on the Dover-Calais link ever since the passing of the fabled 'Golden Arrow' service in 1972. In comparison, it had been noted by the late Brian Langford that the tunnel would simply offer its clientele "a loo and a light bulb". The P&O initiative proved to be a great success and during the May-August period of 1993, bookings rose by as much as 30 per cent. With port check-in times and simplified port procedures, 1993 became the most intensive year yet on the Dover Strait.

The earlier generation of freight ships built for the Zeebrugge link were replaced by the new 'Seaway' class, the *European Trader* finishing in October 1991, the 'Clearway' in August 1988 (latterly running to Boulogne) while the 'Endeavour' lasted until September 1995 after latterly operating on the Calais service and relieving on other company routes. All three were to finish their careers with P&O on the North Channel link.

The joint trading agreement between P&O and the Belgian RMT came to an end on the final day of 1993 after which the Belgians moved their service to Ramsgate and the Finnish-owned Sally Line. This move was not totally unexpected but proved to be the final nail in the coffin of the Belgian state-owned ferry line. They were badly advised and the historic link closed completely in February 1997.

THE JOINT VENTURE

The former Sealink (British Rail) ferry fleet had been acquired by the Bermuda-based Sea Containers in 1984. During this period, much was promised but little was achieved apart from some general interior upgrading of the former

The **P&OSL Picardy** in the livery of the short-lived joint venture between P&O European Ferries and Stena Line. The former **Pride of Free Enterprise** is seen arriving at Calais. (Miles Cowsill)

railway ships. However, in May 1990 the Swedish company Stena Line acquired the business for £259 million and quickly sought to stamp their authority on the routes they operated. Having seriously misjudged the market by opting for a Scandinavian cruise-style culture, the Swedes quickly embarked on Operation Benchmark in order to seek economies and restructuring throughout the business.

Acting on P&O's initiative, Stena Line moved to enlarge their own Dover-based fleet but whereas P&O's ships were purpose built and ideally suited to the Calais service, Stena Line introduced an eclectic collection of vessels, some of which were far from suitable. The inevitable split between Stena and their French partners SNCF occurred at the start of 1996 after which both concerns moved to enlarge their respective fleets creating over-capacity and reduced profits for all concerned.

P&O European Ferries were always the proven market leaders catering mainly for the upper end of the passenger market never failing to remind their public of their history and heritage as the leading British passenger shipping company. Stena's approach in comparison was far more basic with their

Top: The **Pride of Burgundy** *in the joint venture livery prior to being renamed* **P&OSL Burgundy**. *(John Hendy)*

Above: The *Stena contribution to the joint venture,* **P&OSL Provence** *passes the super-freighter* **European Seaway** *off the port of Dover. (FotoFlite)*

intrusive music and fast food outlets; there really was no comparison.

However, Government permission was granted to proceed with a joint venture during November 1997. The agreement also covered the Dover-Zeebrugge and Newhaven-Dieppe routes; P&O would provide eight vessels and Stena five while voting rights would be 60/40 in favour of P&O.

The P&O passenger-carrying ships were all renamed and received the prefix 'P&OSL' instead of 'Pride of'. The exception was the *Pride of Bruges* which became the *P&OSL Picardy*. Meanwhile, the former Stena ships were renamed and repainted in the P&O style, their *Stena Empereur* becoming *P&OSL Provence* while the *Stena Fantasia* became the *P&OSL Canterbury*. The rest of the Stena contributions to the Joint Venture were not renamed and were duly sold for further trading. The joint company house flags adorned the funnels of the new look fleet although a red line along their superstructures between hull and upperworks was a concession to Stena.

One of the first tasks of the new management was to uprate the *P&OSL Provence* and new generators were fitted to provide more light in what was always a rather gloomy ship. She was fast on passage but not being built for the route, performed badly when manoeuvring in port so that attention to her bow-thrust units was also required.

The new company sought to create a 'Brand World' for the fleet which would see standardised fittings and fixtures throughout. The popular waiter service Langan's Brasseries were installed in the former Stena ships as were other P&O style outlets selling food and beverages. Club Class lounges were also introduced which greatly served to raise the on-board ambience of the fleet newcomers.

It was originally planned that the *Pride of Bruges* would serve on the Newhaven-Dieppe route but there were concerns that her draft might be a problem at low water in the River Ouse and in the event, the *Stena Cambria* (ex *St Anselm*) worked the service until it closed in January 1999. The link had also inherited the fast craft *Stena Lynx III*, renamed *Elite*, but this had been promptly dispensed with as being unreliable and prone to delays.

The *Stena Cambria* had operated with a French crew who

were duly moved to the freighter *European Pathway* which was then laid up without a gearbox. This had been transferred to the *P&OSL Burgundy* and finding itself a ship short, the joint venture duly took a four-month charter of the *Stena Royal*. The ship was the former *Prins Filip* which had been the pride of the Belgian RMT but had been laid up at Dunkirk ever since the closure of the Ostend-Ramsgate route in February 1997. It was soon realised that the ship presented the company with a golden opportunity to further improve standards on the Dover-Calais route and after entering service as a freighter on the Zeebrugge link in November 1998, her charter was quickly extended to seven years. An extensive overhaul ensued and renamed *P&OSL Aquitaine* she took up service to Calais in November 1999. Work on her interior was ongoing but her finish was the first indication of the standards expected of the joint venture. Unsurprisingly, it was somewhere between the two – an improvement on Stena but certainly below the standards expected of P&O European Ferries. The arrival of the 'Aquitaine' saw the withdrawal of the 'Picardy' after she had covered the refit period in February 2000. By now the ship was too small and the company had moved on.

During spring 2000, it was announced that the joint venture was to end. P&O were invited to purchase Stena's 40 per cent share for £150 million while Stena would also take over P&O's operation at Felixstowe. For Stena it was a chance to improve its North Sea freight operations while for P&O it was an opportunity to capitalise on the high capacity short-sea business it knew best. Once cleared by the European Commission, the deal was completed during October 2000.

DARWIN PROJECT SIGNALS ZEEBRUGGE CLOSURE

With the closure of the Zeebrugge service as from 15th December 2002, the freighters *European Pathway* and *European Highway* underwent a hefty conversion to passenger ships for the Dover-Calais link. Their conversions were known as 'The Darwin Project'.

The 'Pathway' completed service on 22nd April leaving the 'Highway' to close the link which she duly accomplished with all appropriate ceremony. During its 36 years' operation, the company's Belgian route had come full circle. For a period it had enjoyed huge patronage and had been Dover's premier

*Top: The joint venture's **Stena Cambria** entering Newhaven Harbour from Dieppe. The route was closed in January 1999. (Miles Cowsill)*

*Above: The **Pride of Dover** as she appeared in the modified P&O livery with the white paintwork lowered to allow 'P&O' to be painted larger. (John Hendy)*

Top: The **Pride of Canterbury** (2) is seen leaving Calais. Originally built as the super-freighter **European Pathway**, she was converted with her sister on the closure of the Zeebrugge link in 2002. (John Hendy)

Above: The **Pride of Canterbury**'s simple interior furnishings reflect those of a motorway service station. (P&O Ferries)

freight route. The opening of the Channel Tunnel coupled with the improvement of the coastal motorway system from Calais into Belgium, had been its downfall. Rather than spend four hours travelling to Zeebrugge by ship, it was now possible to save time via Calais, where there was always a ferry waiting for the return sailing, and the excellent motorway connections into the Low Countries. It was most fitting that retired Commodore Jack Dawson was on board for the final sailing and sounded the ship's siren as she left Zeebrugge.

Both freighters were sent to Lloyd Werft at Bremerhaven where their profiles were completely changed in readiness for the second phase of their careers. Passenger accommodation was raised from 200 to 2,000 and as the *Pride of Canterbury* (ex 'Pathway') and *Pride of Kent* (ex 'Highway') the sisters commenced operation to Calais on 12th May and 14th June 2003. The former replaced the briefly styled *PO Canterbury* (ex *Stena Fantasia*) while the latter replaced the *PO Kent* (ex *Pride of Kent*, ex *Spirit of Free Enterprise*) which were duly sold on to Greek owners.

The rebuilt ships undoubtedly contain the best Club Class lounges in the fleet. These are beautifully fitted out areas immediately below the bridge and stretch the full width of the ships. In the best P&O tradition this fully carpeted area is full of comfortable armchairs and sofas with reproductions of heritage paintings around the bulkheads. The rest of the accommodation is light, fitted out as it is in modern, bright functional laminates much as any motorist has come to expect on a break between long periods of motorway driving.

A modification to the ships' livery took place during the 2002-03 round of refits. This involved the lowering of the blue hull paint which served to make the vessels look a little top heavy. It did, however, allow more space to apply the company's website and 'P&O' in rather larger letters than would have previously been possible.

Winter 2003-04 proved to be an extremely difficult period for P&O Ferries who, as part of a wide-ranging business review, now sought to make annual savings of £15 million. Apart from the ongoing threat of international terrorism, budget airlines were making inroads into the established trade and so New Year's Day 2004 saw the remaining freighter *European Seaway* withdrawn from service and three months later, the *Pride of Burgundy* downgraded to freighter status. The rest of the fleet were also to feel the pinch with the majority of on-board services closing during the night.

The 'Seaway' was firstly sent to Falmouth where she acted as an accommodation vessel during the period of fleet overhauls before being offered for sale. Being purpose built, she proved to be such a specialist vessel that no purchasers were forthcoming and in June she sailed for lay-up at Birkenhead where she was removed from the sales list. After a whole year out of service, the 'Seaway' returned to Dover in January 2005 after which the 'Burgundy' also returned to passenger mode. This coincided with the withdrawal of the *Pride of Provence* (ex *Stena Empereur*) just before Christmas 2004 and her almost immediate sale to Greece.

The withdrawal of the *Pride of Aquitaine* followed in May 2006. She was always an expensive ship to operate with charter fees costing in excess of £4 million a year, and in view of the financial difficulties imposed on the company at that time, it made little sense to continue running her. She was quickly acquired by the French company LD Lines and renamed *Norman Spirit* for service between Portsmouth and Le Havre. At the time of writing, greatly changed internally, she is back on the Dover-Calais link operating on a joint DFDS/ LD Lines service.

DP WORLD TAKE THE HELM

The acquisition of the entire P&O Group by DP World in March 2006 left the ferry division in something of a quandary. DP World had, after all, purchased P&O for the vast assets in its ports portfolio but P&O Ferries was given an undertaking that there were no plans to sell off what, after all, was only a very small part of the overall package.

The new owners promised a major investment programme and the first evidence of some long-awaited expansion came in early 2007 with the purchase of the Spanish ro-ro vessel *El Greco*. The ship had been built as the *Midnight Merchant* and had been chartered by Norfolkline for their fledgling Dover-Dunkirk West service on which she commenced service in October 2000. She was eventually replaced by purpose-built tonnage and left Dunkirk in August 2006 for her new base at Barcelona. P&O's new purchase was named *European*

*Top: The English Channel's largest ferry, the **Spirit of Britain** dwarfs the **Pride of Calais** at Dover's Eastern Docks. (Captain Steve Johnson)*

*Above: The **Spirit of Britain** ready for floating out at Rauma, Finland, as the incoming water fills the dry dock in which she was built: June 2010. (John Hendy)*

Spirit of Britain

Endeavour and initially ran as a stern loader between Liverpool and Dublin prior to being made ready for the Dover Strait. With her first commercial voyage taking place on 11th January 2008, the ship supplemented the 'Seaway's' freight sailings allowing a six-ship operation to continue throughout 2008 during the year-long period when the *Pride of Canterbury* was off service. The ship had been seriously damaged after hitting a submerged wreck whilst sheltering off Deal during inclement weather in January 2007.

It was always the company's intention that the new *European Endeavour* would also serve the Irish Sea and the freight downturn saw her laid up at Dunkirk in May 2010 until early the following year. She presently maintains the Liverpool-Dublin link.

TWO NEW SHIPS – ONE NEW ERA

Following many years of speculation, during August 2008, P&O Ferries signed a 360 million Euro contract with Aker Yards in Rauma, Finland (later renamed STX Europe) for the two largest ferries ever to be constructed for any English Channel route.

After a period of careful consideration with their new owners, P&O Ferries were able to start afresh at designing a pair of ferries for the 21st century without any of the restrictions which would have been imposed by the P&O Group. They were in a position to start again from scratch in designing specialist ferries for a uniquely specialist trade. For the first time the company were given a clean sheet of paper enabling all those involved to look at the construction of the vessels in a completely new light. So often in the past, new builds had simply been larger and more luxurious versions of what had gone before but here, for the first time, this fresh and open-minded approach provided a number of ground-breaking, and even unique, advances in ferry design. Among these is the hull form which was formulated following extensive tank tests and which provides for a completely new

*Left: The **Spirit of Britain** leaving Calais. The ship not only introduced a white funnel to the fleet but embraces many new and innovative features which place her at the forefront of ferry design and safety. Her funnel extension pipes have since been raised. (John Hendy)*

Top: The Brasserie on board the **Spirit of Britain**. *(P&O Ferries)*

Above: The wall murals in the new ship's after lounge are designed to capture the 'Spirit of Britain'. (P&O Ferries)

design for a water depth of up to 30 metres.

At 47,592 gross tons and 213 metres in length (as opposed to the 169 metres of the *Pride of Dover*), the two ferries are 'Dover Max' (the largest that the port can handle) and the first designed to manoeuvre under their own power in 50-knot winds. Accommodation is for 180 freight vehicles on twin decks (representing 2,750 lane metres), more than doubling the capacity of the 'Chunnel Beaters' *Pride of Dover* and *Pride of Calais* which have been totally eclipsed and outclassed in every aspect of their design. A third vehicle deck allows up to 195 tourist cars (in an extra 1,000 lane metres) to be stowed and should the planned new ferry ports at Dover and Calais ever be constructed, space has been allocated in the ships' shell plating to allow a side door to be inserted. Two well-furnished passenger decks above allow a certificate for 2,000 people. The designers have attempted to supply something for everyone and all is furnished using the company's colour palette of the blue and white of Portugal and the yellow and red of Spain, as seen on the house flag.

Commercial lorry drivers have their own dedicated space, 'Routemasters', with a self-service restaurant, shower room/ toilets, television/ music area, sun loungers and even their own area of outside deck space. The Club Class lounge is situated at the ships' after end and although smaller than some, has the added advantage of its own area of outside deck which is certainly a first for the company. Adjacent to this is the Brasserie with its P&O heritage posters reminding diners of the company history.

In order to celebrate the 2012 London Olympics, it was originally announced that the new ships were to be named *Olympic Spirit* and *Olympic Pride* but it was later realised that these choices would have raised objections from the Olympic governing body. Safer names were therefore selected and on 9th June 2010 the *Spirit of Britain* was floated out of her dry dock and, following her fitting-out and trials in the freezing Gulf of Bothnia, completed her maiden voyage on 21st January 2011. The *Pride of Dover* had finished service on 14th December 2010 and was sent to Tilbury to lay up pending sale.

Although due in service in September 2011, the *Spirit of France* did not operate her maiden commercial voyage until 9th February 2012 after vibration problems experienced on

*The first arrival of the **Spirit of France** in January 2012. (John Hendy)*

trials had delayed her delivery. Soon after her arrival, the 'Britain' was also returned to Rauma to receive work to dampen a similar defect.

The new ships very much set the trend which all others must follow. They are claimed to be the safest and most environmentally friendly vessels in the Channel and although there was initially an option to build two further ferries of the same class, in a period of recession this looks increasingly unlikely. Indeed, had the present twins been ordered two or three months later than they were, the necessary finance would have been far more difficult to raise and they may well have not been built.

It had originally been intended to withdraw the *Pride of Calais* at the time that the *Spirit of France* entered service in September 2011 but her late arrival kept the earlier ship on station, mainly in a freight mode but also as a full passenger

vessel during the peak period of 2012.

Overcapacity in the Dover Strait and the downturn in freight crossing the Channel saw the *European Seaway* withdrawn from service for the second time at the end of September 2011 when she went to lay up at Tilbury. However, the failure of SeaFrance saw her return to soak up the excess traffic on 17th November. Her subsequent departure on a four-month charter as an accommodation vessel linked to the construction of a wind farm off the Lincolnshire coast in April 2012 was a new venture for P&O Ferries and one which kept the 'Calais' on station longer than had been expected.

The ferry industry moves on and with the new *Spirit of Britain* and *Spirit of France* in service, P&O Ferries has re-established itself and stamped its authority as market leader in the Eastern Channel.

Chapter 2

The Normandy & Iberian routes

NEW THINKING ON THE WESTERN CHANNEL

The origins of P&O operations in the Western Channel go back to 1964 when the entrepreneurial Norwegian businessman Otto Thoresen commenced a new and revolutionary ferry service linking Southampton and Cherbourg. Otto Thoresen had crossed the English Channel from time to time and was unimpressed by the services then operated by the British and French nationalised railway companies. His famous words, "You needn't be a genius to do better than this" were indeed prophetic. He observed that both England west of Dover and France west of Boulogne were without any roll on service at a time when the port of Southampton was looking for a new operator to fill the place in the Outer Dock vacated by the withdrawal of British Railways' service to the Channel Islands.

In the early sixties, fortune took a hand for Otto Thoresen. Firstly, at Southampton, British Railways withdrew their long-established Channel Islands passenger service concentrating all traffic at Weymouth on the former rival route established by the old Great Western Railway. It was also known that British Railways wished to terminate their overnight service to Le Havre, which had been losing money for years. The St Malo night crossing was also under scrutiny and there were those who even foresaw the complete abandonment of Southampton as a railway port.

Across the Channel, at Cherbourg, they were also experiencing problems with a slow, but inevitable, drop in passenger traffic. The great French port had been a calling place for many of the trans-Atlantic liners but as air traffic made increasing inroads into the Europe-USA market, so Cherbourg began to look elsewhere towards its future prosperity.

Working on behalf of Otto Thoresen, the London firm of shipbrokers, James Burness & Sons Ltd, entered into negotiations with Southampton, Weymouth and Cherbourg, concerning a possible new ferry service. In January 1963, 'Lloyd's List' was able to announce that a Norwegian group, with British and other interests, were planning to start a service in the spring of the following year. The 'other interests' in the new group were the Paris-based freight company,

Top: The **Viking I** *at Thoresen Car Ferries' original berth at the Outer Dock Southampton. (Ferry Publications Library)*

*Above: On 10th March 1965 the **Viking III** was launched at Lubeck, West Germany. (Ferry Publications Library)*

Top: The aft end of the Promenade Deck with the aircraft-type seating and cabins, on the right. (Ferry Publications Library)

*Above: The Smugglers Cave bar on the **Viking I** was based on the design of a traditional British pub. (Ferry Publications Library)*

Worms et cie.

In early April 1963, it was announced that shipyards in Britain, France, Germany and Scandinavia had been asked to tender for the line's new ship, the order eventually going to Norway, on price and credit considerations. The service was to be known as the 'Southampton-Cherbourg Car Ferry Service' and on 15th April it was stated that the new ship had been ordered on behalf of a new company – Otto Thoresen Shipping Company A/S. Meanwhile full agreement had been reached, between Southampton Docks and Cherbourg, for a new car ferry service between the two ports.

Prior to the arrival of Thoresen Car Ferries, 3rd September 1963 saw the British Railways Board finally declare their intention of closing the 120-year-old Le Havre passage as from 1st May of the following year. It was claimed by British Railways that the Le Havre service had lost £1 million since the previous attempt to close it, that there was no collusion with the new company and that they did not seek closure because the *Normannia* was required at Dover. For the Southern Region of British Railways, Mr R.E. Sinfield said, "If we cannot make it (the service) pay, we feel as custodians of national money that we should economise. We are just as much businessmen as anybody else."

Mr David McKenna, the General Manager of the Southern Region, said, "We have studied the alternatives and Newhaven is not only better suited geographically but promises a better economic return." (Note: British Railways started a car ferry service from Newhaven to Dieppe in June 1964 using the former Southampton-St Malo passenger steamer *Falaise*. The route was left to the French in January 1985.)

Thirty-four objections to closure were heard but finally, as expected, the Minister of Transport (Mr Ernest Marples) approved British Railways' application but only on the understanding that their service continued until the new Thoresen service began. Meanwhile, the General Steam Navigation Company was to start a new twice-weekly service carrying freight between Southampton and Le Havre.

Otto Thoresen was left to pick up the pieces which the Nationalised company had left and the order for the first Thoresen ship was made before British Railways sought to withdraw. The Le Havre route was very much an afterthought

Above left: The **Viking I** *arrives at Southampton for the first time from her builders. (Ferry Publications Library)*

Above right: This view shows the **Viking I** *at her lay-by berth at Le Havre as the* **Viking IV** *arrives at the port on her first commercial sailing from Southampton. (Ferry Publications Library)*

Left: The **Viking II** *is pictured here at Newcastle during her Round-Britain Showing the Flag Cruise in autumn 1964. (Ferry Publications Library)*

Above: The **Viking II** *makes an impressive view inward bound to Southampton off The Needles, Isle of Wight. (Ferry Publications Library)*

and Otto Thoresen expressed no interest in it until BR decided to withdraw. Thereafter, the local authorities gave Thoresen the same enthusiastic backing that his company had received at Cherbourg.

THE VIKINGS ARE COMING

During the last quarter of 1963, plans for the new Southampton-Cherbourg route gathered pace and on 19th September a second ship was ordered while negotiations for an additional service to Le Havre were underway.

The second vessel was ordered on the strength of early bookings and the tremendous enthusiasm on both sides of the Channel and in Norway. In order to help finance the second ship, the company raised its share capital from 7 to 12.5 Kr – each ferry costing approximately 23 million Krona or £1.5 million. (In the event the ships cost £1.2 million each.) At a meeting in Oslo on 25th September, shareholders were given the first details of the twin ferries.

Each would carry 180 cars on two decks. Eleven lanes of cars would be driven on at the stern in Southampton and off through the bow in France – the first drive-through in ships to serve our shores. Eight hundred passengers (300 in sleeping accommodation) would be carried on the four-and-a-half hour crossing (actually 940 passengers and a five-hour crossing) and the ships would be driven by two Swedish-built Pielstick engines of about 11,000 hp (10,200), which would turn two variable-pitch propellers able to be controlled directly from the bridge. The first ship was to be delivered on 2nd April, the second in July. As a safety measure, their hulls would be coloured bright orange, deckhouses would be an anti-glare green while the rest of the superstructure would be white.

The two ferry terminals were already under construction and a credit had been arranged for 80 per cent of the cost of the two ships, repayable in eight years. More information about the new Norwegian service was forthcoming in early November 1963. The first ferry was to start on 11th May while the second ship was expected on 1st August. Forty-five minute turn rounds (later retimed at an hour) were aimed at and fares

*Left: The **Viking II** at speed in the Solent during her second season on the English Channel. (FotoFlite)*

*Above: An impressive photograph of the **Viking I** showing the full extent and wealth of outside deck space on this early Thoresen ship. (Ferry Publications Library)*

*Above right: An evening view of the Princess Alexandria Dock showing the ro-ro freighter **Viking IV**, which was able to offload straight onto the quay, while the **Viking I** waits for her night sailing to Le Havre. (Ferry Publications Library)*

*Right: Thoresen Car Ferries gained tremendous publicity from the shipment of parts of Concorde. This view shows part of the main fuselage of the plane going on board the **Viking II**. (Ferry Publications Library)*

*The **Viking II** arriving at the entrance to the Solent inward bound from Le Havre in Townsend Thoresen livery in May 1969. (Ferry Publications Library)*

were fixed at £2.17s.6d. (£2.87) for an adult single, while children under 14 were priced at £1.10s.6d. (£1.50). Single car rates were £4.10s.0d. (£4.50) for vehicles up to 11 ft long and £1 extra for vehicles up to 12 ft 6 inches. Cycles would also be carried for 10s.0d. (50p). All these fares were considerably cheaper than those of British Railways yet Mr Thoresen stated that his company was not trying to start a fare-war.

At a press conference in London on 5th November, it was finally announced that the two ships would be named *Viking I* and *Viking II*. They would offer first-class liner standards and cars would be able to drive off at the rate of one every 4.5 seconds. Unloading would be achieved in 13 minutes.

The order to build the first two 'Viking' ships went to Kaldnes Mek Verksted at Tonsberg on Oslofjord. The *Viking I*'s keel was laid in October 1963 and she entered the icy waters of the fjord for the first time, shortly before noon, on the following 31st January – just 18 weeks later.

The *Viking I* was finally delivered at Tonsberg on 29th April but before being handed over, she was given a last trial run on Oslofjord. In fog and rain she managed to clock 20.5 knots – one knot faster than her designed speed.

It was announced that she would enter service four days ahead of schedule on 7th May instead of 11th May and to quote Otto Thoresen again, "Because everything has worked so smoothly and efficiently, we are now able to start our ferry service to the Continent four days ahead of schedule and this still allows us the seven days which we would like to work up the ship, the crew and the ports to maximum efficiency, before we start handling passengers and cars. We are particularly grateful to the ports of Southampton and Cherbourg, where the new installations and buildings are being completed in record time." Meanwhile, on the 30th April, the *Viking II* was launched.

On 4th May, the *Viking I* was given a practice loading with

70 cars that were provided with full documentation for the drivers in order to test the arrangements and to discover any hidden snags. This was repeated twice more before the ship entered service. The following day the vessel gave a five-hour press cruise in the Solent while another press trip, this time to Cherbourg, was arranged for 6th May.

With everything having gone so smoothly until this time, it was unfortunate that a mechanical problem should now occur, which was to cause a slight blemish in the festivities. On arrival back from the French port that evening, the *Viking I* was 40 minutes late with the port engine running hot.

The maiden voyage was postponed for three days as a result of some technical problems. It was hoped to have the ship ready for Sunday 10th May but in the event it was Monday 11th – the originally planned date.

The ship was timetabled to leave at 10.30 and the company were honoured to have the Mayor of Southampton cut a tape before walking down the linkspan into the ship followed by his official car. One hundred and seventy cars were carried on the first five-hour crossing and with an hour's turn-round in Cherbourg, she left again at 16.30. This pattern continued until 15th May when some night sailings were introduced.

In the first three operating weeks, Thoresen Car Ferries carried 13,000 passengers and 3,500 cars. Bookings already showed that a profit would be made; yet British Railways had claimed that their service lost them £173,116 a year. During the whole of 1962, British Railways had carried just 72,190 passengers and 2,642 cars.

THE 'VIKINGS' MAKE AN IMPRESSION

From the start, Thoresen set out to offer a friendly service making a Channel crossing a pleasant experience instead of just another tiresome journey. In early July 1964 the decision was made, at a board meeting in Oslo, to order a third ferry for the following season – this, after just two months of operation. The order, at Lubeck in West Germany, would be made straight away and Otto Thoresen stated that the third ship would give the company greater flexibility and enable them to cope with the anticipated increase in traffic. One national newspaper suggested that the *Viking III* could be used as a relief ferry on other routes and Santander (Spain) was

*The French-registered **Leopard** inward bound to Southampton from Le Havre. (FotoFlite)*

*Top: P&O Normandy Ferries' British-registered **Dragon** opened the rival service to Townsend Thoresen Car Ferries operation in July 1967. (Ferry Publications Library)*

*Above: The **SF Panther** at Southampton linkspan prior to taking up service in November 1973. (Ferry Publications Library)*

suggested as a possibility.

The *Viking II* was delivered at Tonsberg on 15th July and entered service four days later, on the Cherbourg link. There was no great news coverage or celebration concerning her arrival – she simply slipped into her timetable and on the following day (20th July) allowed the *Viking I* to formally open the Southampton-Le Havre service.

On 25th September the British Railways steamer *St. Patrick* made her final crossing from Southampton to St Malo, thereby ending the railway association with passenger sailings from the port. It was now left to private enterprise.

In 1964 Thoresen Car Ferries carried 192,274 passengers and 55,139 cars although Southern Region experts still believed that the Norwegians would eventually abandon the Le Havre route. Thoresen Car Ferries' success was put down to four reasons, firstly the attractiveness of the new ships, the frequency of the service, cheaper fares than previously and finally reluctance of motorists from the Midlands and the West to pass through London to Dover.

Meanwhile, the *Viking III* entered in June 1965. From the start Thoresen looked at route expansion. Winter service across the River Plate was investigated but prevented by an unstable political situation in Argentina. Plymouth-Spain was also mooted but instead off-season charters were found for at least one vessel while the other two continued with reduced crossings from Southampton. In June 1967, continued expansion saw the freight-only ro-ro vessel *Viking IV* take up service to Le Havre.

After four years of operations in June 1968, Thoresen Car Ferries was taken over by George Nott Industries Ltd of Coventry – the owners of Townsend Car Ferries at Dover. The merger provided a much stronger operations unit and provided considerable scope for improvements in operational efficiency. As far as the general public were concerned things remained the same as usual, although after 1976 the Townsend fleet at Dover adopted the Thoresen orange hull livery. The merger produced the European Ferries Group and during November the *Viking II* was transferred to the Dover-Zeebrugge link for six weeks while the *Free Enterprise II* became a regular addition to the summer Cherbourg sailings as from 1970 until 1974.

P&O SOUTHERN FERRIES AND NORMANDY FERRIES

Following the British Rail withdrawal from Le Havre, the P&O subsidiary, the General Steam Navigation Company (GSNC) had operated a limited cargo service on the route. However, the success of the Thoresen venture prompted them to enter into a partnership with the French company, Societe Anonyme de Gerance et d'Armement (SAGA) and two similar style vessels were ordered from Ateliers et Chantiers, Nantes for delivery in spring and winter 1967. The joint company was to be known as Normandy Ferries.

As originally planned, the twins were to have been freight only roll on–roll off ships but it was soon realised that the service stood a far greater chance of success if the summer holiday trade was also catered for, in spite of the new operation by Thoresen Car Ferries. Although the new ferry service was to trade as Normandy Ferries, the first ship the British-flagged *Dragon* was provided by Southern Ferries, a wholly owned subsidiary of the General Steam Navigation Company (GSNC) while the second, the *Leopard* was owned by SAGA, and was French crewed and French flagged. The name for the British vessel came from the mythical creature adorning the ancient coat of arms of the Kingdom of Wessex, while a *Leopard* appeared on the arms of Normandy crest.

The ships cost just under £2 million each and boasted excellent accommodation for 850 passengers, while their stern-only loading garages accommodate some 250 cars. A waiter service restaurant was provided for 70 diners in addition to a 163-seater cafeteria. Cabin berths were provided for 276 and there were 156 reclining chairs with additional saloon seating for a further 320. At 18 knots, the sisters would be able to cross the Channel in seven hours which was much slower than the Thoresen ships.

After some delays, the *Dragon* was eventually launched on 26th January 1967, entered service on 7th July and took up service on 29th June. In her first season she offered a 22.30 sailing from Southampton with an 11.30 return.

On 3rd July, Princess Alexandra officially opened the old Outer Dock for ferry traffic and the basin was renamed in her honour. Prior to the *Leopard*'s arrival, Normandy Ferries

planned a weekly crossing from Le Havre to the Irish port of Cobh but this was later modified to Rosslare after disagreements between Cork Harbour Commissioners and Irish Shipping who were to be partners in the new venture. The *Leopard* was launched on 3rd December 1967 and entered service the following May. She duly opened the new Rosslare link on 1st June leaving Le Havre at 12.15 on Saturdays, arriving at Rosslare at 10.15 the following day. The return crossing left Rosslare some two hours later for a Monday arrival in Le Havre at 10.00. The Irish service was very successful and 15,000 passengers and 4,000 cars (an average of 110 per crossing) were conveyed before the service closed for the season. Both ships were used in the following year when the service became twice weekly.

It was soon very apparent that the Le Havre route could not maintain a full profitable winter service, with both Thoresen Car Ferries and Normandy Ferries on the route. Thoresen had built their vessels with the winter charter market in mind and now Normandy Ferries tackled the winter lull in a totally different manner. During the *Dragon*'s first refit (when the service to Le Havre was covered by the chartered Dutch cargo vessel, *Lea*) her accommodation was modified. In the forward lounge on B Deck, the tables and chairs were stripped out and a dance floor was created. The St George's Bar became a nightclub and 96 extra berths, in two-berth cabins were built on her open vehicle deck, aft. All this was in readiness for the new off-season 'Sunshine Route' from Southampton to Lisbon (Portugal) and Casablanca (Morocco), which started on 24th November 1968.

Although the *Leopard* only had a passenger certificate for 250 for this first sailing, she was fully booked within 24 hours of its announcement. Between November 1968 and May 1989, a trip was offered every 11 days, although during the French General Strike, in early June 1968, the *Dragon* ran two sailings from Southampton-Rosslare-Lisbon with a passenger certificate for 272.

During the winter of 1968/69, the *Leopard* offered sailings from Rouen-Southampton-Lisbon-Casablanca, having now been built with the modifications to her accommodation as her sister. So hopeful were P&O that the new service would really take off, an order was made for a large new cruise ferry, the

*Top: The launch of the **Viking Venturer** on 1st June 1974 at Aalborg Vaerft, Denmark. (Ferry Publications Library)*

*Above: Following the introduction of the **Eagle** on their Iberian services, P&O Southern Ferries subsequently withdrew the vessel in October 1975 due to lack of traffic from the UK. (Ferry Publications Library)*

Eagle, which was due for delivery in March 1971. Until the *Eagle*'s delivery, the *Dragon* and the *Leopard* continued the off-peak service operating every 11 days during the winter of 1970. The Casablanca sailings were never very popular and some were curtailed, with Lisbon becoming the southern terminal later. A fare of the day (including meals) was £19 from Southampton to Lisbon. From mid-June to mid-September the extra services were suspended when there was money to be made on the English Channel. A typical timing was as follows: Monday 11.00 depart Southampton, Wednesday 13.00 arrive Lisbon, Wednesday 17.00 depart Lisbon, Friday 19.00 arrive Southampton.

The new *Eagle* was now due to enter service on 2nd April 1971, offering three trips each fortnight to Lisbon and Casablanca with one sailing extended to Tangier. The Lisbon service was due to become year-round and in the run-up before the entry of the *Eagle*, the *Leopard* was scheduled to make the final Normandy Ferries sailings. However, with the new ship late from the builders, the *Dragon* was called in to operate an extra round trip to Tangier in early April 1971. Finally, the new Southern Ferries vessel entered service on 18th May and then it was announced that the *Dragon* and *Leopard* were also to be withdrawn from the Rosslare service as from 11th October. It was stated by P&O at the time that the route was profitable but the decision had been made to keep the twins in service on the route for which they were built, as there were signs at last of year-round traffic building up. With the ships no longer tied up on the long-haul to Ireland, no fewer than 40 per cent more sailings could now be offered on the Le Havre service and such was the build-up in freight that a chartered vessel, named the *Falcon* was acquired.

The Normandy Ferries withdrawal from the Irish route prompted their partners, Irish Shipping, to seek their own vessel and when this was eventually found. During the overhaul periods of the *Dragon* and *Leopard* in 1979 and 1980, Irish Continental as they became known, chartered their *Saint Patrick* and *Saint Killian* to cover the Southampton-Le Havre service.

The next expansion for P&O at Southampton was to acquire the *Peter Pan* in order to start yet another new twice weekly to

San Sebastian, Spain. She duly refitted in Le Havre and entered service on the new 29-hour service on 22nd December. The climate was not then right at the time for further expansion and the *Eagle* was withdrawn from service in October 1975; the *SF Panther* followed shortly afterwards and both routes were closed. The *SF Panther* then transferred to P&O's operations to Shetland and Orkney as the *St. Clair*.

Following the venture of Normandy and Southern Ferries into the Spanish market at Southampton; the service continued with the *Dragon* and *Leopard* offering two sailings a day in each direction for the next nine years, until P&O Normandy Ferries was taken over by their rivals Townsend Thoresen in 1984.

THE SUPER VIKINGS

In December 1970, details of a major European Ferries building programme involving five new ships was announced. Dover was to receive two more vessels in the successful 'Free Enterprise' series (*Free Enterprise VI* and *Free Enterprise VII*) while Southampton would receive three larger Viking vessels – 'Super Vikings' – which, it was assumed, would be named *Viking V*, *Viking VI* and *Viking VII*. The new ships ordered for Southampton were to be modelled on the original Thoresen 'Vikings' but with the influence of the 'Free Enterprise' class ships. This was evident with the internal layout of the passenger accommodation with the introduction of open plan lounges first adopted in the original *Free Enterprise* back in 1962. The five ships were to cost over £20 million and had all three 'Super Vikings' been allocated to Southampton then it is likely that the original vessels would have been replaced much earlier than they were. Southampton was now handling in the region of 130,500 vehicles and 475,000 passengers a year by the end of 1970 and with further demand for more passengers and car space on the Le Havre and Cherbourg routes, the new 'Super Vikings' were designed to fill the growing demand in the Western Channel. The new class of vessel was designed to carry 1,200 passengers and 275 cars on two decks, with cars loading at the side via a ramp to the upper deck at Southampton and unloading in France via an internal ramp within the vessel to the main deck. With their arrival some five years later, the company was able to boast their largest ever

vessels in service on the cross-Channel routes.

Meanwhile, Dover's *Free Enterprise II* was back at Southampton on 30th April 1970 to repeat her summer sailings while the *Viking IV* was moved to Dover in early July to assist on the Zeebrugge route. The Atlantic Steam Navigation Company provided the *Cerdic Ferry* from Felixstowe to replace her. With the 'FE II' finishing her seasonal stint on 19th September, it was all change once again for the other two ships, which both returned to their respective stations.

The *Viking III* returned to A/S Larvik-Frederikshavn for the winter of 1971-1972, leaving Southampton on 20th September, but during that period both the 1964 twins were needed to maintain the twice-daily service.

The European Ferries Group further expanded on 18th November 1971 when it acquired the Atlantic Steam Navigation Company for £5.55 million. In 1972, three 'Vikings' were required between 16th June and 17th September and the 'FE II' was back from Dover to assist them between 19th May and 24th September. Her move westwards again meant a switch for the *Viking IV* and the *Cerdic Ferry*.

In 1974, the *Free Enterprise II*'s summer Cherbourg season was reduced and operated only from 27th June until 1st September. All three 'Vikings' were required from 25th May until 29th September but there were now question marks placed over this happy arrangement when the first two 'Super Vikings' were launched in Denmark during June and October, since the *Viking Venturer* and *Viking Valiant* were both destined for Southampton. In early October, the *Viking II* left Southampton for the company's new passenger service linking Felixstowe and Zeebrugge, which she started on 23rd October.

The first 'Super Viking' class ship was not named *Viking V* as originally assumed but *Viking Venturer*. The 'Venturer' was launched on 1st June 1974 by Mrs Ustered Svenson, wife of the Chairman of the original Thoresen car ferry company. The external appearance of the new 'Viking' and her Danish sisters which were to follow over the next 17 months, included twin-funnels, as with the early 'Vikings', with inside facilities for passengers on four deck levels. The passenger accommodation on the 'Super Vikings' was upgraded compared with the new-building 'Free Enterprise' ships for Dover. Their passenger facilities included on D Deck an

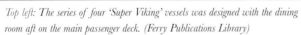

Top left: The series of four 'Super Viking' vessels was designed with the dining room aft on the main passenger deck. (Ferry Publications Library)

Top right: The main passenger accommodation on the 'Super Viking' ships was modelled very much on that of the Dover vessels with high-capacity aircraft-style seating in stark contrast to the original Thoresen ships. (Ferry Publications Library)

*Above: This view shows the **Viking Venturer** arriving in the Solent for the first time on her delivery voyage from Denmark. (Ferry Publications Library)*

*Above: A four-berth cabin on the **Viking Venturer**. (Ferry Publications Library)*

Entrance Reception from the car decks with a Ticket Office, Immigration Room and toilet facilities situated on both the port and starboard sides with stairs then leading up to C Deck. Forward on D Deck was the main cabin accommodation that was far superior to that in earlier 'Vikings'. There was far more space available for passengers and a wider choice of cabins designed for the overnight sailings and cabins suitable for day sailings. Interestingly, only a few of the four-berth cabins offered en-suite facilities, which meant that most passengers had to leave their cabins to visit the 'bathroom'.

C Deck (Main Deck) was devoted entirely to passenger lounges and included gift shops, duty-free shops and an Information/Purser's office. The passenger lounge comprised semi-reclining seats with a partitioned bar area off the main lounge with comfortable seating for 100 persons. At the after area on C Deck was the cafeteria. The space abaft of this was originally devoted to a luxury restaurant with seating for 162 persons, which included a bar and dance floor. The restaurant areas in the 'Venturer' and 'Valiant' were later moved to the starboard side, next to the cafeteria, in order to offer more seating space for passengers.

From midships on C Deck, stairs led up to B Deck where further cabins were originally designed. In the first two 'Super Vikings' these cabins were removed in the 1980s to provide a 'Club Class' lounge for those passengers wanting some peace and quiet away from the open lounges of C Deck.

The main car decks on the original 'Super Vikings' were able to accommodate 125 cars with a further 105 cars which could be driven onto hydraulically operated car decks above them. A further 50 cars could be loaded in an enclosed garage at the aft end of D Deck. The flexibility given with the car decks enabled the main car deck to be used for lorries, coaches and caravans while the other car decks could be used for small vehicles.

ENTER THE VIKING VENTURER

The *Viking Venturer* entered service on 22nd January 1975 under the command of Captain Tony Shopland on the Le Havre run operating with the *Viking III*, which released the *Viking I* for charter work. Passengers were immediately impressed with 'Venturer' and particularly by her public rooms and the

internal design. Southampton was also very pleased with its new ship, especially with her superior cabin accommodation.

The *Viking Valiant* was launched during October 1974. Townsend Thoresen decided to introduce her to the newly opened Felixstowe-Zeebrugge service to boost both passenger and freight space. The *Viking Valiant*, which had originally been destined for Southampton, arrived at the Suffolk port on 21st May 1975 to join the *Viking II* on service.

From 1976 a gradual progress of transferring the sailings from Southampton to the new ferry port at Portsmouth started, with Townsend Thoresen opening a new link from this port to Cherbourg. On the return of the *Viking I* from Felixstowe she was renamed *Viking Victory* after HMS *Victory* Nelson's famous flagship, which was the centre piece of the city's naval heritage nearby to the ferryport. Chairman, Keith Wickenden said that the decision to rename the ship was a gesture to the people of Portsmouth who had welcomed the new service to the city. Portsmouth not only saved an hour at sea but it offered excellent road communications with a spur of the M27 leading into the new port. The new terminal also lacked the fierce and militant trade union practices, which had

The **Viking Victory** *opened the Portsmouth-Cherbourg service in May 1976. She is seen here leaving Portsmouth in her first season. (Miles Cowsill)*

all but strangled Southampton. The *Viking Victory* opened the new service on 17th June, offering two round sailings a day until 12th September.

The 'Super Vikings' did not go to Portsmouth in its first year as a ferry port but from 1977 they did commence sailings there when one of the 'Super Vikings' was transferred at peak weekends to operate to and from Le Havre as an experiment. The pattern of these new sailings meant better utilisation of the ships for the company with the shorter crossing time to Portsmouth. One of the 'Super Vikings' departed from Le Havre at 09.00 and arrived at Portsmouth at lunchtime, enabling her to sail back to the French port at 14.30 ready for the night sailing to Southampton. This proved a great success and from 1978 the company then gradually scaled down their operations at Southampton in favour of the new port.

The *Viking Valiant* formed part of the Queen's Silver Jubilee Spithead Naval Review in June 1977. Two years later, on 17th May 1979 the *Viking Victory* (which had made the inaugural crossing to Cherbourg in 1964) celebrated the 15th anniversary of the opening of the Thoresen Car Ferries service between Southampton and Cherbourg. The ship conveyed a party of guests who were entertained to lunch by the local Chamber of Commerce; the group included 15 members of the original Thoresen staff still working at Southampton.

In 1980, the major cross-Channel ferry operators had to contend with the French fishermen's blockade of the Channel ports and Townsend Thoresen at Southampton and Portsmouth had their sailings affected very badly at the height of the holiday season. The *Viking Valiant* spent 32 hours at sea trying to get into a French port and the *Viking Venturer* 26 hours, having to return after trying to get into Cherbourg first and then St Malo. The *Viking Victory* was to take even longer than the 'Super Vikings' when she spent 55 hours at sea before arriving back to Portsmouth without unloading. The *Free Enterprise II*, which was serving on the Portsmouth-Cherbourg link at the time, finally ran the gauntlet of the French fishermen when, on Sunday 17th August, she was able

*Left: The **Viking Venturer** inward bound from Le Havre during her first season on the English Channel. (FotoFlite)*

to break the blockade of trawlers at the entrance to the terminal at Cherbourg and finally tied up with the aid of frustrated motorists who drove off dockers and fishermen from the quayside. The *Viking Venturer* and *Viking Valiant* broke the blockade at Le Havre in the dead of night whilst the fishermen were caught off their guard.

By 1981 Townsend Thoresen decided to transfer the morning Cherbourg sailing of the 'Super Vikings' from Southampton to Portsmouth and with this transfer Portsmouth was now offering up to five sailings a day during the peak season to the French port.

In early spring 1982, the Falklands War broke out and provided major problems for Townsend Thoresen as the company were faced with three ships being requisitioned for the Task Force. The *Free Enterprise V*, which was going to replace the *Viking Victory* on the Cherbourg link in 1983, was brought into service early on the Southampton-Le Havre freight run in April on the departure of the *Europic Ferry* for the South Atlantic.

JUMBOISATION

Townsend Thoresen decided to withdraw their passenger/car ferry operations from Southampton as from 1st January 1984 in favour of Portsmouth, leaving only their freight sailings behind. Freight sailings would have been moved at the same time but there was not enough storage for freight at Portsmouth. However, some 12 months later, all services were withdrawn from the famous port.

Compared with their earlier sisters the 'Super Vikings' all enjoyed fairly quiet careers and there was never much time for charter work as they were all used on a year-round basis on their routes.

During December 1984 Townsend Thoresen announced that the *Viking Venturer* and *Viking Valiant*, together with two of the 'Free Enterprise' class ships would be enlarged to meet the increasing demand for freight space on the Le Havre and Zeebrugge routes. The two 'Super Vikings', like the *Free Enterprise VI* and *Free Enterprise VII*, would be fitted with larger forward sections as well as being horizontally cut in two with an additional full-length vehicle deck inserted, enabling, in the case of the 'Venturer' and 'Valiant', to carry 60 lorries

*Top: A rare view of the **Viking Valiant** pictured at Caen during a press trip when Townsend Thoresen were considering opening a new service to the port of Ouistreham. (Ferry Publications Library)*

*Above: In sub-zero conditions the aft section of the **Viking Venturer**'s passenger accommodation is lifted during her jumboisation. (Ferry Publications Library)*

*Left: An impressive view of the **Viking Venturer** and **Free Enterprise V** in the English Channel. (Ferry Publications Library)*

after jumboisation. Schichau Unterweser AG of Bremerhaven was appointed to carry out the conversion works with the *Free Enterprise VI* being the first to sail to Germany in June for the conversion, followed by her sister in October. The 'Super Vikings' underwent their conversion during an eight to nine month period in the winter of 1985/1986.

Meanwhile, during December 1984 P&O Ferries had transferred their services from Southampton to Portsmouth, a move that was prompted by yet another period of dockers' industrial unrest. Then on 4th January 1985 P&O announced that they had sold their interests on the English Channel (Dover-Boulogne and Portsmouth-Le Havre) to European Ferries for £12.5 million. The merger of P&O Normandy Ferries and Townsend Thoresen solved one of the problems at Portsmouth with the pending summer season; the *Free Enterprise V* would not be available for the Cherbourg route as she was required on the Dover-Zeebrugge link, while the two 'Free Enterprise' ships underwent jumboisation.

The former P&O sister ships, the *Dragon* and the French-registered *Leopard*, were quickly brought under Townsend Thoresen management and were included in the schedules of the company at Portsmouth for the forthcoming season. During the summer, they covered all the Le Havre sailings with the charter roll on–roll off freighter *Viking Trader*, while the 'Super Vikings' covered the Cherbourg route.

In October 1985, Townsend Thoresen decided to convert their Felixstowe-based freight ships, *Baltic Ferry* and *Nordic Ferry* to multi-purpose passenger/freight ships for the Felixstowe-Zeebrugge service at a cost of over £9 million each. The conversion would allow for the transfer of these ships to the Zeebrugge route, which in turn would release the *Viking Voyager* and *Viking Viscount* so they could be transferred to Portsmouth to operate with their jumboised sisters. On the arrival at Portsmouth of the former Suffolk 'Vikings' the *Dragon* would be transferred to the Cairnryan-Larne service while the *Leopard* would be withdrawn. The

*Right: The **Viking Voyager** passes Dunnose Point, Isle of Wight outward bound to Cherbourg. This view shows her with the P&O house-flag on her funnels prior to the demise of the Townsend Thoresen brand name in October 1987. (FotoFlite)*

END THORESEN

VIKING VOYAGER
DOVER

*Top: The **Dragon** arrives at Portsmouth in Townsend Thoresen livery following the takeover of the company in 1986. She was later transferred to the Irish Sea services. (Ferry Publications Library)*

*Above: P&O Portsmouth introduced their own fast ferry service to Cherbourg in 1999 using the **Superstar Express**. (Ferry Publications Library)*

French crew were not happy over the withdrawal of the *Leopard* and they blockaded the ramp at Le Havre over the inevitable redundancies. Eventually the company agreed to transfer the French crews to the *Viking Viscount* and put her under the French flag.

After the launch of the new hull sections for the 'Super Vikings' at Bremerhaven during late October into the River Geeste (they were launched as one unit end to end), they were then towed to dry dock for separation. Schichau Unterweser started work on the *Viking Venturer* in December 1985. During the weekend of 4th/5th January, the first section of her superstructure was lifted from the existing hull in sub-zero conditions that made work extremely difficult. Unlike the 'Free Enterprise' twins, the superstructure of the 'Super Viking' class had to be lifted in two operations, as the passenger accommodation was much larger. The delicate lifting of the aft section of the 'Venturer' took about four hours. The forward section was then removed and left with the aft section on the quay, ready for the next part of the operation. The new bow section was then joined to the existing hull of the 'Venturer' and an extra car deck was constructed after the final forward bow section had been removed. Then, after the hull had been joined together, the superstructure was placed onto the joined hull sections and the builders undertook the delicate task of joining everything up again!

P&O ACQUIRE TOWNSEND THORESEN

The *Viking Venturer* underwent sea trials after her conversion on 6th/7th May and sailed to Portsmouth on 14th May. After a brief call at the port, the 'Venturer' sailed to Southampton for further work to her passenger accommodation. On 19th May, the *Viking Venturer* returned to Portsmouth to take up the 15.00 sailing to Le Havre.

The *Viking Venturer* was now looking a very different ship and rather dwarfed her newly arrived sister from Felixstowe. The new linkspans were not completed until early July and so the *Viking Venturer* was put on the midday sailing to Cherbourg until the arrival of the *Viking Valiant* from Germany. The 'Valiant' entered service on 3rd July on the 23.30 sailing to Le Havre; her jumboised sister, the *Viking Venturer*, had been transferred a week earlier to the Le Havre link. The smaller

The **Pride of Bilbao** arriving at Portsmouth from Spain. The new ferry operation to Spain opened in April 1993 and closed in October 2010. (Ferry Publications Library)

*Top: The **Pride of Winchester** leaves Cherbourg on her afternoon sailing to Portsmouth in her last season on the English Channel. (Miles Cowsill)*

*Below left: An impressive view of the **Pride of Portsmouth** leaving Le Havre on her afternoon sailing to Portsmouth. (Miles Cowsill)*

*Below right: The **Pride of Hampshire** leaves Portsmouth on her morning sailing to Normandy. The jumboised 'Super Vikings' were transferred to the Cherbourg link on the introduction of the former Olau ships on the Le Havre service. (Ferry Publications Library)*

'Vikings' were then transferred to the Cherbourg route.

On 5th December 1986 Townsend Thoresen (European Ferries) was acquired by the P&O Group. The major impact of the takeover was seen some ten months later with the demise of the Townsend Thoresen name. For the 1987 season all four 'Super Vikings' appeared in a slightly different livery from that of the previous year with the funnel colours in pale blue and with the P&O house flag. On 21st October 1987 the Townsend Thoresen name disappeared and was replaced with the branding of P&O European Ferries. As from 1988 all four 'Super Vikings' at Portsmouth appeared in the new P&O European Ferries livery with dark blue hulls and funnels and incorporating the house flag on their twin funnels.

The *Viking Venturer* was renamed *Pride of Hampshire* and her operating sister on the Le Havre route, the *Viking Valiant*, was renamed *Pride of Le Havre*. The two twin sisters, the *Viking Viscount* and *Viking Voyager*, on the Cherbourg route were respectively renamed *Pride of Winchester* and *Pride of Cherbourg*.

By 1990 it was becoming increasingly evident that the now jumboised 'Super Vikings' were too small for the Le Havre route and the company were starting to look for replacements for these vessels. Already their rivals, Brittany Ferries, had ordered two jumbo ferries to compete with P&O.

Continued growth of freight traffic by 1992 saw the former Dover-based freighters *European Clearway* and the *European Trader* operating on the Le Havre route as the company had failed to secure suitable tonnage for the service. For 1993, P&O were confident they had acquired new tonnage for the Le Havre service from Viking Line but in the event they were not successful in securing the *Athena* and *Kalypso* and it was to be another 12 months until suitable tonnage could be found.

In April 1993, the company expanded their operations at Portsmouth with a new service to Bilbao in Spain using the former Viking Line vessel *Olympia*, which was renamed *Pride of Bilbao* for her new role. Prior to this new service, Brittany Ferries from Plymouth had operated the only UK-Spain link. The new operation was an overnight success for the company attracting not only good car loadings but also growth in the mini-cruise market, with passengers able to enjoy three nights at sea from Portsmouth.

Following the demise of Olau Line services between Sheerness and Vlissingen, P&O European Ferries were successful in acquiring the relatively new vessels *Olau Hollandia* and *Olau Britannia*. Whilst the 'Olau ships' were not ideal for the route, they did herald an expansion of their operations on the Le Havre route in the light of Brittany Ferries' continued refurbishment and renewal programme of their fleet. The former 'Olau ships' emerged as the *Pride of Portsmouth* and *Pride of Le Havre*. The arrival of the new ships for the Le Havre service saw the transfer of the jumboised 'Super Vikings' to the Cherbourg route and the withdrawal of the smaller original Felixstowe 'Super Vikings'.

The *Pride of Winchester* was the first of the former 'Felixstowe Vikings' to be withdrawn from service and she completed her last sailing between Portsmouth and Cherbourg on 8th July 1994. She was subsequently sold to Greek interests and sailed from Portsmouth on 27th July, renamed *V Kornaros*. Meanwhile, the *Pride of Cherbourg* was sold to Lineas Fred.Olsen and renamed *Banaderos* for service in the Canary Islands.

P&O FERRIES ERA

Following the introduction of the former 'Olau' vessels, P&O European Ferries were to see a 24 per cent increase in traffic on the Le Havre route but despite this new tonnage the company were to face substantial losses on all their routes over the next couple of years. Their rivals, Brittany Ferries, continued their rapid growth and expansion with new ferries, and ever-increasing passenger numbers were attracted to the French operation from P&O. The heavy financial losses, mainly due to the high charter fees of the *Pride of Portsmouth* and *Pride of Le Havre*, and failure to introduce new tonnage on the Cherbourg route, was eventually to see reorganisation of P&O's operations in Britain in an attempt to stem losses within the ferry group.

Prior to this reorganisation, Portsmouth management were successful in securing the *Isle of Innisfree* from Irish Ferries for their Cherbourg operation. Again, like the former 'Olau ships', she was not really suitable for her new role as she lacked any substantial cabin accommodation. The Irish vessel underwent an extensive refit and overhaul for her new role on

Top: The **Pride of Cherbourg** *leaves Portsmouth during her last season on the service. (Miles Cowsill)*

Above: Under the command of Captain Tony Shopland, the **Pride of Portsmouth** *leaves her homeport for Le Havre in May 2001. (Miles Cowsill)*

the English Channel as replacement to the now 27-year old, jumboised 'Super Vikings'. She was renamed *Pride of Cherbourg* and entered commercial service on 12th September 2002. Meanwhile, the former *Pride of Cherbourg* was sold to El Salam Shipping Company as the *El Salam I*. Her sister, the *Pride of Hampshire* was also sold to the Egyptian company and made her last commercial sailing with P&O on 25th September. During the career of both these 'Super Vikings', at Southampton and Portsmouth, they were to carry more than 50 million passengers and sail over five million miles.

As part of the reorganisation of P&O's operations in the UK, the offices at Portsmouth were closed and all operations were moved to Dover. Given the new approach to the new branding of P&O Ferries, modification to all the ships' liveries took place during the 2002/2003 refits at Portsmouth, to bring all the fleet in line at Dover and on the North Sea passenger operations. This involved the lowering of the blue hull paint, to allow more space to apply the company's website and a large 'P&O' lettering to both sides of the ship.

P&O Ferries also undertook an extensive refit to the *Pride of Portsmouth* and *Pride of Le Havre* to bring the on-board facilities in line with that of the ships at Dover, including the branding of Langan's brasserie restaurants on board. The *Pride of Bilbao*, operating the Spanish service, also underwent a major million pound refit and also the various restaurant brands on board the ship were remodelled on the Langan's brand. The *Pride of Cherbourg*, operating the Portsmouth-Cherbourg service, underwent a major overhaul as well, including a Langan's and an improved club-class lounge. Additional cabins were not offered to the ship at the time but there were plans in her next refit to undertake this work.

In the light of continued expansion by Brittany Ferries, P&O Ferries decided to offer a rival fast ferry service between Portsmouth and Caen in 2004 using the chartered *Max Mols* which was renamed *Caen Express*. The vessel was a near sister to that of the *Cherbourg Express*, which had been employed on the Portsmouth-Cherbourg route since April 2000. She was able to carry 800 passengers and 220 cars.

The 2004 season saw P&O Ferries' operations at Portsmouth offering no fewer than nine sailings to France a

day

Top: The **Pride of Cherbourg** *(ex **Isle of Innishmore**) was introduced on the Cherbourg service in 2002. (Miles Cowsill)*

Above: P&O Ferries opened their rival service to that of Brittany Ferries to Caen using the **Caen Express**. The Danish-registered chartered vessel is pictured here leaving Portsmouth. (Miles Cowsill)

Right: The **Cherbourg Express** leaves Portsmouth on her morning sailing to Cherbourg. The InCat craft was later transferred to the Irish Sea on the demise of P&O's operations to France. (Miles Cowsill)

*The **Pride of Portsmouth** makes a fine sight as she leaves on her afternoon sailing from Portsmouth to Le Havre in June 2005. (Miles Cowsill)*

during the peak season and two round sailings per week to Spain. The fast ferry operation to Caen proved very successful with extremely good loadings on the route, carrying some 8,000 passengers during the first three weeks of operation.

On 28th September 2004, P&O announced that they would withdraw from the Western Channel the following season. Despite increased passenger numbers, the operations from Portsmouth were continuing to make heavy losses. As part of this announcement P&O indicated that they had been in discussions with their rivals Brittany Ferries to bring the *Pride of Le Havre* and *Pride of Portsmouth* under their management. The new ships would operate under Brittany Ferries' management and would be renamed *Étretat* and *Honfleur* but would remain under the British flag. There would be no such joint arrangement for the Cherbourg route, which

would be closed and the *Pride of Cherbourg* laid up for further charter work. The *Cherbourg Express* would be transferred to the North Channel and the *Caen Express* returned to her owners. The *Pride of Bilbao* operations to Spain would continue as the company felt the service could be made profitable in the long term and they were also committed to the charter of the vessel until 2010.

During early December the Office of Fair Trading (OFT) decided not to give the green light to P&O's proposals and the handover of the Le Havre service to Brittany Ferries. The decision of the OFT was to result in Brittany Ferries withdrawing their interest in taking over the service. In the event P&O Ferries continued the Le Havre service until the following September with the Cherbourg service closing on 2nd January 2005.

*The **Pride of Le Havre** leaves Portsmouth during her last season on the English Channel before the demise of the Le Havre service. (Miles Cowsill)*

On 30th September the *Pride of Portsmouth* and *Pride of Le Havre* closed the Portsmouth-Le Havre route after 42 years of operation since Otto Thoresen established it in 1964. The chartered vessels were returned to their owners and eventually were disposed of for further service in the Mediterranean. The Portsmouth-Le Havre route was immediately taken over by LD Lines with their *Norman Spirit* (ex *Prins Filip*, ex *Stena Royal*, ex *P&OSL Aquitaine*, ex *Pride of Aquitaine*) the following day. Since P&O's withdrawal, the service has seen mixed fortunes.

The *Pride of Bilbao* continued to soldier on with the 36-hour link to Spain from the UK for the next five years. The decision was made in 2010 to close the operation as the charter of the vessel was coming to an end with her owners, Irish Ferries. In spite of looking for suitable replacement tonnage and restructuring of the service, the management at Dover could see no way that the service could be made profitable in the future. The *Pride of Bilbao* completed her last sailing to Spain on 25th September 2010, closing a chapter of 46 years of British and Norwegian operations on the Western Channel.

The influence of the opening of the Channel Tunnel was to have a greater impact than originally envisaged on the Western Channel operations and with continued competition from the Dover Strait, both from the Channel Tunnel and the ferry operations, more rationalisation is on the horizon for the current near monopoly French operator.

Chapter 3

The North Sea Connections

HULL-ROTTERDAM (EUROPORT) AND ZEEBRUGGE
MAKING A START

Until the mid-1960s, motorists from Scotland, the Midlands and from Northern England, were forced to travel to south east ports in order to cross the English Channel and North Sea. While the Essex port of Harwich provided regular links with Scandinavia and the Low Countries, even this was inconveniently placed for many UK citizens.

At this time, the well-established and nationalised Associated Humber Line (AHL) operated a traditional lift on–lift off service from Hull's Riverside Quay to Rotterdam (Parkhaven) with the modern motor vessels *Bolton Abbey* and *Melrose Abbey* maintaining the link. Apart from unit loads, some cars were transported and the ships carried as many as 80 passengers in one class.

With commercial traffic on the increase and every indication that this trend would continue into the foreseeable future, it was at this point that P&O's Ian Churcher saw the opportunity of operating a ro-ro service between Hull and Rotterdam, not just for freight but also for passengers and their vehicles. A consortium of six companies was duly formed (two British, two German and two Dutch) in which P&O's General Steam Navigation Company held a 35 per cent share. Shortly before the new service commenced, the two British concerns, the General Steam Navigation Co. and Tyne Tees Steam Shipping Co., were merged giving the P&O Group a 45 per cent share in the new route.

Twin overnight ferries were constructed by AG Weser at Bremerhaven and on 17th December 1965 the British-flagged *Norwave* entered service on the 197-mile route leaving port at 18.00 with arrival at 08.00. She was a compact and extremely functional vessel of 3,692 gross tons, with capacity for just 249 passengers and 70 cars in addition to 47 x 12-metre freight units. Her Dutch-flagged sister ship *Norwind* followed her into service on the following 22nd March. Unusually, the vessels' twin vehicle decks were of double height thereby allowing freight to be carried on both by use of internal lifts while both bow and stern doors were provided for easy loading. The early public relations material described the route as the 'Sleepway to Europe' and during the first year's operation as many as

*Top: The launch of the **Norwind** at AG Weser's yard at Bremerhaven prior to the ship entering service in March 1966. (Ferry Publications Library)*

*Above: The **Norwind** and **Norwave** had capacity for just 249 passengers. Here is the **Norwave**'s appropriately named Snug Bar. (Ferry Publications Library)*

40,000 passengers were carried: by 1987 this had risen to 500,000.

The new North Sea Ferries operation was worked from Hull's King George V Dock and Beneluxhaven within Rotterdam's massive new Europort dock area. The addition of the second ship allowed NSF to offer a daily service in each direction every night of the week from 1967 onwards and the service quickly prospered at the expense of the rival AHL operation.

The ships quickly proved popular with passengers who enjoyed their intimate ambience but there soon became times when they were capacity constrained not only during the busy tourist season but also on a year round basis for freight. Their diminutive size actually meant that they were restricting growth and although the short-term answer was simply to charter spare ro-ro and lo-lo ships to help shift the spare commercial traffic, it soon became obvious that the *Norwind* and *Norwave* would require replacement by larger ships. As far as the passengers were concerned, the great attraction of the service was that their £12 return ticket offered not just a passage but included a cabin, an evening meal, morning tea and breakfast. Whilst some still doubted whether the new service could ever be made to pay, Ian Churcher and his NSF board soon knew that they were onto a winner!

ADVANCES

It came as no surprise when NSF ordered a pair of second-generation ships which were a huge advance on the earlier pair and were duly named the *Norland* (British) and *Norstar* (Dutch). New berths were constructed on either side of the North Sea along with improved passenger facilities and extra standage room for freight. Built again by AG Weser Seebeckwerft in Bremerhaven, the ships were 12,988 gross tons and carried 1,243 passengers, 139 x 12-metre freight units or 500 cars. As the NSF service to Europort involved no less than eight hours in port, speed of cargo handling was not essential and the ships were therefore built as stern loaders, internal lifts carrying lorries and trailers to the twin decks above the principal vehicle deck.

*Left: A sparkling new **Norwave** at speed in the North Sea. (FotoFlite)*

Top: The **Norwind** *alongside the Leopold II Dam Terminal at Zeebrugge in May 1985. (John Hendy)*

Above: The **Norwind** *and* **Norland** *representing the first two generations of North Sea Ferries, alongside at Europort. (Ferry Publications Library)*

The *Norland* entered service on 10th June 1974 allowing the smaller *Norwave* to commence a new passenger service to Zeebrugge (Prins Filipsdok). Very wisely, the company had placed their ro-ro vessel *Norcape* on the route some 18 months previously in order to create a freight base for the new multi-purpose link and the introduction of the cascaded vessels from Hull was therefore seamless. Meanwhile, the new *Norstar* took up the Europort route on 19th December 1974 after which the first-generation *Norwind* joined her sister on the Belgian route.

The far greater passenger capacity of the new ships allowed tour operators in the Midlands and North of England to exploit the Europort crossing and the route was to become an extremely popular venue for weekend excursions with a full range of on-board entertainment being offered.

Ian Churcher retired from NSF in May 1975 when he was made Executive Chairman of P&O Ferries. His leadership and commitment to the service was exemplary and he was duly awarded an OBE for services to the transport and shipping industries. His place as Chairman of NSF was taken by the Dutch representative, Jaap Feringa who in turn handed over to Graeme Dunlop in 1979. Mr Dunlop was eventually promoted to become Chairman of P&O European Ferries.

Although originally a consortium run by six companies, in 1981 NSF became a 50/50 operation between the P&O Group and the Dutch Royal Nedlloyd Group.

NORLAND IN BATTLE

In April 1982, the *Norland*, under the command of Captain Don Ellerby, was requisitioned by the Ministry of Defence and joined the Task Force for the liberation of the Falkland Islands. The ship became a troopship carrying 900 men of the 2nd Parachute Regiment and sailed 8,000 miles into the war zone via Sierra Leone and Ascension Island.

Suddenly finding themselves a ship short, the NSF management hastily looked for a replacement and on 25th May, the 5,149 gross ton Viking Line vessel *Viking 6* was taken on charter. With a capacity for just 600 passengers, 100 cars and 22 freight units, she was no match for the absent *Norland* and during summer 1982, the company certainly experienced capacity problems on the Europort link.

Following the Argentine surrender and the end of hostilities in the South Atlantic, it was hoped that the *Norland* would soon be returned to her owners. However, she had proved herself invaluable during the conflict and the MOD therefore retained her to run the 3,500-mile ferry service between Ascension Island and the Falklands. This continued for a further six months and so in November 1982, the Irish Continental Line's *Saint Patrick II* (7,984 gross tons) was chartered to take over from the *Viking 6*.

The *Norland* finally left Port Stanley on 6th January 1983 and returned to Hull 24 days later having steamed 66,093 miles. Following the appropriate welcomes, the rust-streaked ship retired to dry dock at Immingham where she was once more prepared for commercial service in a multi-million refit lasting some 11 weeks. On 19th April she was back on station.

After ten years in service, it was decided to uprate and upgrade the *Norland* and *Norstar*. The work started with their internal fixtures and was mainly carried out during their port time without removing them from service. This all culminated in their stretching by 20.5 metres during 1987.

The Zeebrugge service was running to capacity with the charter of the German freight vessels *Wuppertal* and then *Fuldertal* but turn round times were slow as the Prins Filipsdok was entered through a system of lock gates. Late in 1984, a large, purpose-built, new Leopold II Dam Terminal was opened on the Mole in the port's outer harbour which not only eased matters but also served to improve the company's profile. The freighters were replaced by the larger 91 x 12-metre trailer capacity *Thomas Wehr* and *Gabrielle Wehr* during January 1986; their entry into service giving the Belgian link 50 per cent more freight capacity.

THIRD-GENERATION

Plans were now announced for the construction of a pair of third-generation cruise ferries each costing £40 million. Although originally planned to build them simultaneously in British and Dutch yards, the removal of Government subsidies from Van der Giessen-de Noord, near Rotterdam, saw Nedlloyd turn to Japan for their vessel.

The first of the new generation ferries was launched by HM Queen Elizabeth the Queen Mother at Govan Shipbuilders on

*Top: The **Norwind** and **Norland** are seen in the King George V Dock at Hull. (Ferry Publications Library)*

*Above: In 1987, the **Norland** and **Norstar** were stretched by 20.5 metres. (Ferry Publications Library)*

*Top:The freight ship **Norcape** (ex **Tipperary**, ex **Puma**) is seen leaving Zeebrugge for Teesport. (Miles Cowsill)*

*Above: Alongside the Leopold II Dam Terminal at Zeebrugge, the **Norland** is seen in her revised NSF livery. (Ferry Publications Library)*

9th September 1986, the largest and the last significant British flag ferry ever built in the UK. She was the largest passenger ship built in Britain since the Cunard Line's *Queen Elizabeth 2* in 1969. Following the launch of the *Norsea*, 11 days later her sister, the *Norsun*, was launched at Nippon Kokan KK at Yokohama. With a beam of 25.38 metres, the twins were the largest vessels capable of passing through the lock into the King George V Dock at Hull allowing just 27cm (less than a foot!) either side.

During 1987, North Sea Ferries adopted a completely new livery for their ships. Gone were the compass logo and the familiar black hulls and orange funnels in favour of a Dutch inspired twin-tone blue livery with matching funnel logo. In preparation for the relaunch of the Zeebrugge service following the arrival of the new ships, the *Norland* and *Norstar* were both to be sent back to their builders at Seebeckwerft, Bremerhaven for major ship surgery in which they were lengthened by 20.5 metres with the insertion of a new amidships module.

The new *Norsea* suffered minor delays at Govan and bad weather postponed her sea trials in the Firth of Clyde so that she did not operate her maiden voyage until a month later than originally planned, on 8th May 1987. The *Norsun* commenced service four days later. Their arrival in service allowed the earlier twins to sail to Bremerhaven and their arrival back allowed the disposal of the first generation *Norwind* and *Norwave*. By now they were hopelessly outdated with their passenger capacity for just 249 passengers and such a small freight capacity that the company were forced to charter in expensive ro-ro units to accommodate all the traffic on offer. Ending their services on 5th July and 30th June respectively, the ships were soon sold to Ventouris Lines of Greece being named *Grecia Express* and *Italia Express*.

The arrival of the third generation of North Sea Ferries coincided with the opening of Hull's new £5 million ferry terminal by Princess Margaret on 15th July 1987. General Manager Remi Speld called 1987 a "landmark year for the company".

STRETCHED

The stretched *Norland* and *Norstar* now boasted a gross

*Top left: The third generation **Norsea** undergoing trials in the Firth of Clyde. (Ferry Publications Library), Top right: The Dutch-flagged **Norsun** is seen leaving the New Waterway on her overnight crossing to Hull. (John Hendy), Above left: The Dutch-flagged **Norstar** manoeuvres in the King George V Dock at Hull. (Miles Cowsill), Above right: The **Norland** at speed in the North Sea. (Ferry Publications Library)*

*The **Norbank** and her sister **Norbay** were built for the new 'North Sea Express' freight service between Hull and Europort in 1993 and 1994. (Miles Cowsill)*

tonnage of 26,919 and cargo space had been increased by 20 per cent (to 179 x 12-metre trailers or 500 cars) thereby equalling that of the new ships. During the revamp of their passenger areas, accommodation had been lowered to 881 but this was deemed to be quite sufficient especially as it was more than three times larger than that in the ships that they were replacing.

As the *Norsea* and *Norsun* were both the largest ships that could be accommodated by Hull's King George V Dock, it was known that any future-generation vessels would have to berth elsewhere. Although the dock represented a safe haven away from the strong tidal flows and range of the adjacent Humber estuary, berthing there at some states of the tide could prolong an overnight journey apart from adding unnecessary

stresses on the ships' engines. In 1992, the port owners, Associated British Ports, therefore gained powers to build a new terminal and three river berths adjacent to the King George V Dock while in response to this, NSF ordered two super-freighters from the Dutch yard Van der Giessen-de Noord.

The rationale behind the new 'super freighters' *Norbay* and *Norbank* was to provide a new express freight service between the new River Terminal and a brand new berth at Europort. With the advent of the Channel Tunnel there was a concern that traffic throughout the UK would be drawn towards the shortest crossing and that other, longer, routes would suffer as a consequence. The new 22-knot NSF service would offer a three-hour later departure time and yet still berth on the other side at 07.00 the following day. Traffic trends were changing and more drivers now accompanied their lorries on the longer crossings. With space on the three freight decks for 156 x 12-metre trailers, the ships also boasted accommodation for as many as 114 drivers. In the meantime, the company chartered the ro-ro freighters *Norcove* and *Norcliff* (ex *Fichtelberg*) to carry excess freight on the Europort link.

The new 'North Sea Express' service finally commenced on 31st October 1993 with the 17,474 gross tons Dutch-flagged *Norbank* followed on 28th February the following year by the British ship *Norbay*.

In order to bring them up to SOLAS 90 regulations, more upgrading was carried out to the Zeebrugge ships *Norland* and *Norstar* during early 1994. The main work involved damage stability but new propellers, anti-fouling paint and a restaurant revamp were also forthcoming. New longitudinal

bulkheads below decks meant a loss of space amounting to 20 per cent. The ships were out of service for five weeks and two 60-trailer ro-ro ships were chartered to cover the Zeebrugge service in their absence. It was planned to retain the vessels to cover for the loss of freight space in the passenger ships but they proved unsuitable and so the new 'super freighters' were called in to run a weekend shuttle service to the Belgian port. In July NSF chartered the French flag *Saint Louis* which, with her 70-trailer capacity, operated on alternate days through until October.

Displaced from the Ipswich link, the *Norcape* was moved to the Hull-Zeebrugge crossing during April 1995 but traffic results indicated that there was insufficient traffic for a two-ship operation and the smaller *Merchant Victor* was therefore withdrawn from the service at the end of August.

The first of the fourth generation was the **Pride of Rotterdam**. *(Miles Cowsill)*

Top: The Dutch-registered **Norbank** *alongside at Europort. (Miles Cowsill)*

Above: The Continental Café on board the **Norsun**. *(Miles Cowsill)*

P&O NORTH SEA FERRIES

It was announced on 17th September 1996 that the P&O Group had purchased the 50 per cent share in NSF held by their partners Dutch Royal Nedlloyd Group for £25.5 million and that with effect from 1st January 1997, both NSF and P&O European Ferries (Felixstowe) Ltd would in future trade as P&O North Sea Ferries. This inevitably meant a change of livery and for the first time, the former North Sea Ferries fleet wore the P&O house flag on their funnels.

With demand continuing to grow, news of the fourth-generation ferries was announced in January 1999. The £90 million ships were ordered from the Fincantieri yard in Venice for delivery in 2001 and represented a completely new design philosophy for the Hull-Europort route. Although a passenger capacity of 1,360 was a slight increase on that of the third-generation *Norsea* and *Norsun*, the huge increase in vehicle deck space would theoretically allow the company to make huge savings by withdrawing the 'super freighters' *Norbay* and *Norbank* whilst operating a similar 22-knot schedule thereby cutting the crossing time by 2 hours 30 minutes. Three vehicle decks would accommodate 3,400 lane metres in addition to 1,500 lane metres for double-stacked container units and a specially designed car deck for 250 tourist vehicles. Tremendous expectations heralded the arrival of the new ships which not only were to be the world's largest cruise-ferries but also the best appointed.

The first of the new futuristic-looking ships, the Dutch-crewed *Pride of Rotterdam*, was handed over to P&O North Sea Ferries on 12th April 2001 and was later named by HM Queen Beatrix of the Netherlands. She left Europort on her maiden commercial voyage on 30th April. The displaced *Norsun* made her final sailing to Europort on 29th April before undergoing a major refit to prepare her for the Zeebrugge service. She emerged two months later replacing the *Norstar* which went for lay-up pending sale although a bow-thruster problem with the new *Pride of Rotterdam* saw the *Norstar* back on the Europort port link for five days in early July.

The arrival of the *Pride of Rotterdam* also displaced the super-freighter *Norbank*, which after a brief visit to Felixstowe, returned to support the new cruise-ferry on 19th

Top left: The **Pride of Rotterdam**'s a la carte restaurant. (P&O Ferries)

Top right: HM Queen Beatrix of the Netherlands, Lord Sterling and the Senior Captain on the bridge of the **Pride of Rotterdam**. (P&O Ferries)

Above: The Irish Bar on board the **Pride of Rotterdam**. (P&O Ferries)

Right: The **Pride of Rotterdam** is towed along the Canale della Giudecca at Venice towards the Adriatic Sea. (P&O Ferries)

*The **Norsea** was renamed **Pride of York** in January 2003. (Frank Lose)*

June although it was the company's original intention to use her at the Suffolk port to replace the *European Tideway* and *Pride of Suffolk*. She was back at Felixstowe during mid-August replacing both the *Pride of Suffolk*, which sailed to Hull prior to transfer to the Irish Sea, and the 'Tideway' which was laid up.

Meanwhile, the *Pride of Hull* was named by Mrs Cherie Blair, wife of the Prime Minister, in her home city on 30th November and sailed on her maiden voyage on 2nd December 2001. Her arrival in service allowed the 'Rotterdam' to proceed to dry dock to receive further attention to a troublesome bow thrust unit during which time the *Norsea* covered her sailings. She was then scheduled to sail to Bremerhaven for a major

refit during mid-December but this was delayed when unexpectedly she sailed to Middlesbrough for a short stint on the Europort freight service.

The *Norsea* returned to traffic on the Zeebrugge link on 1st March 2002 when the Falklands veteran *Norland* was finally withdrawn from service. With a Parachute Regiment band on the quayside, streamers, sirens and with Sir Rex and Lady Hunt (the former Falklands Governor and his wife) in attendance, the occasion was certainly not one to be easily forgotten. Both she and her Dutch sister were duly sold to the Italian company SNAV who used them on the service linking Naples and Palermo (Sicily) until they were broken up in India late in 2010. The original plan to place the super-freighters

Norbank and *Norbay* at Felixstowe was modified and in January 2002 they sailed instead to the Irish Sea which meant a return to service for the *European Tideway*.

P&O FERRIES

A further company rebranding took place in 2002 when P&O North Sea Ferries simply became P&O Ferries which involved the North Sea, Dover and Portsmouth operations. The following January the *Norsun* was renamed *Pride of Bruges* and the *Norsea* became the *Pride of York* with a number of important managerial functions being transferred to Dover. Both the *Pride of York* and *Pride of Hull* transferred to the Bahamian flag in 2011 to avoid new European employment laws that could impose increased wage costs.

The success of the North Sea Ferries operation had been made possible by providing a series of quite distinct purpose-built passenger and vehicle ferries for the Europort route which duly cascaded to the secondary Zeebrugge link. Each pair in the series had grown the traffic to such an extent that a number of chartered ro-ro freighters were hastily required at different times to cater for the remarkable increase of traffic.

The introduction of the supplementary fast 'super freighters' in 1993/94 was a brave and sensible move forward, allowing a much later time of departure with a traditional arrival time without the constraints imposed by the King George V Dock at Hull. By 2001, this strategy was modified with the launch of the *Pride of Rotterdam* and *Pride of Hull* which were intended to accomplish the work for four ships. It was unfortunate that at the time of their introduction, rival freight services were developing on the south bank of the Humber which served to deflect some traffic away from the established route.

THE FELIXSTOWE CONNECTION

The Suffolk Port of Felixstowe can trace its origins back to the 1870s when local entrepreneur and landowner Colonel George Tomline began an ambitious scheme to develop the surrounding area. The first move was to build a 13-mile railway line from neighbouring Ipswich, which opened in 1877, and construct a dock on which work commenced two years later to the south of the town on the banks of the River Orwell.

*Top: The Port of Tilbury with the **Bardic Ferry** at the ASN berth. (Ferry Publications Library)*

*Above: Cars being driven off the **Bardic Ferry** at Tilbury. (Ferry Publications Library)*

*Top: The **Cerdic Ferry** was built at Troon in 1961 and was followed by her sister **Doric Ferry** in 1962. They allowed ASN to operate daily services to Antwerp and Rotterdam. (Ferry Publications Library)*

*Above: The comfortable Lounge Bar on board the **Cerdic Ferry**. (Ferry Publications Library)*

The same year saw the incorporation of the Felixstowe Dock & Railway Company and the new dock was first used to unload a shipment of coal in April 1886.

In the period before the Great War, ship breaking became an important industry while the Royal Navy and later the RAF selected the area as a seaplane base. By the end of the Second World War, Felixstowe Dock was badly silted and trade had fallen away. Following the calamitous East Coast floods in January-February 1953, it was some time before trade began to revive with the provision of greater storage space coupled with good labour relations and a workforce who were ready to accept new working methods. Felixstowe began to blossom at the expense of London and one of the shipping companies that transferred its operations from Tilbury was the Atlantic Steam Navigation Co's Transport Ferry Service (TFS).

THE ATLANTIC STEAM NAVIGATION CO.

The TFS was the brainchild of Lt. Colonel Frank Bustard who before the war had planned to operate a cheap, no-frills, trans-Atlantic service – hence the company's name. The war intervened and it was not until 1946 that Bustard chartered three tank landing craft from the Ministry of Transport for a military service linking Tilbury with Hamburg. This continued until 1955 after which Antwerp became the principal continental port.

In the meantime, in May 1948 a civilian service had commenced linking the Lancashire port of Preston with Larne in Northern Ireland. As we have seen elsewhere, the TFS services were quick to prove themselves but in April 1954 the company was nationalised and taken over by the British Transport Commission (BTC).

Until 1957, all operations in the North Sea and Irish Sea were carried out by a fleet of former tank landing ships that proved to be ideal for the overnight carriage of the commercial traffic of the day and which also included berths for 12 drivers. However, in 1957 the BTC ordered a pair of revolutionary vessels from the yard of William Denny & Bros of Dumbarton. These were the world's first true roll on–roll off freight ships; the *Bardic Ferry* (2,550 gross tons) and *Ionic Ferry* (2,548 gross tons) that joined her sister in the following year.

Another pair of sisters appeared in 1961/62 when the

*The **Gaelic Ferry** entered service in 1964 and was later stretched to increase vehicle capacity. She opened the new link to Europort in 1965. (Ferry Publications Library)*

Cerdic Ferry and *Doric Ferry* joined the fleet and their arrival allowed the company to commence a new daily service to Antwerp and Rotterdam in April 1962. Gradually the old tank landing craft were withdrawn and in January 1964 the introduction of the Swan Hunter built *Gaelic Ferry* (2,760 gross tons) allowed further increased schedules.

In July 1965, the 'Gaelic' opened a new route between Felixstowe and Rotterdam (Europort) and some six months later, the Antwerp service was also switched to the Suffolk port thereby reducing the crossing time from 16 to just 8 hours. This made much sense allowing both greater fleet flexibility and a significant reduction in fuel costs. In August 1966, at a Hamburg auction the company acquired a former United States Navy vessel which was renamed the *Celtic Ferry* to fill the gap prior to new tonnage being introduced. Based at Felixstowe throughout her brief ASN career, the ship was laid up and sold in 1974.

The final ship built for the TFS was the *Europic Ferry* (4,190 gross tons) which entered service between Felixstowe and the new port of Europort on 17th January 1968. The Tilbury connection was finally severed some nine months later.

TFS management had already been involved with English Channel operators Thoresen Car Ferries through the winter charter of their *Viking I* during the period of fleet refits in both sectors of their operations. The first occasion had been in spring 1966 when the *Viking I* was used on both the Tilbury-Antwerp and Felixstowe-Rotterdam links, a pattern which she again followed in December that year. Following the Townsend takeover of Thoresen in 1968, the newly formed European Ferries Group also worked closely with TFS and in November 1971, the then Conservative Government sold the Atlantic Steam Navigation Co. and its subsidiaries to the EFG for £5.5 million.

Top left: The **Europic Ferry** *goes down the ways into the River Tyne. She entered service from Felixstowe in January 1968, several months before the end of ASN's Tilbury connections. (Ferry Publications Library)*

Top right: The **Europic Ferry**'s *spacious Lounge Bar. (Ferry Publications Library)*

Above: Felixstowe with the **Gaelic Ferry** *alongside and the* **Europic Ferry** *arriving. (Ambrose Greenway)*

*The **Europic Ferry** with an upper deck full of trailers. (Ferry Publications Library)*

PASSENGER LINK

Until now the services from Felixstowe had been aimed entirely at the freight industry but in October 1974, a new service was opened to the Belgian port of Zeebrugge which complemented the route operated from Dover. The company's *Viking II* opened the service and was joined by the new Aalborg-built 'Super Viking' *Viking Valiant* (6,386 gross tons) on 21st May 1975. Both vessels maintained the link until the second 'Super Viking' *Viking Voyager* entered service in January 1976 which allowed the 'Valiant' to sail to Southampton while the *Viking I* took the place of her sister. With the arrival of the final 'Super Viking' *Viking Viscount* in May, the services of the small *Viking I* were no longer required and she was returned to Southampton.

On the Europort link, the first of four new double freight decked roll on–roll off vessels entered service on 9th June 1975. This was the *European Gateway* (3,335 gross tons) which

was built by Schichau Unterweser at Bremerhaven. In order to serve the company's North Channel link, the ship was stretched at Amsterdam by 15.7 metres in September 1980 thereby increasing her gross tonnage to 4,263 and her passenger capacity from 132 to 326.

In 1976, the European Ferries Group took over operations at the Port of Felixstowe when they purchased the Felixstowe Dock & Railway Company. A twice-daily service to Zeebrugge had been in operation since 1974 and expansion quickly followed allowing a new purpose-built passenger and freight terminal to be opened in 1978. In the previous year, the former TFS ships were rebranded and repainted in the Thoresen orange.

During October 1977 the *Viking Viscount* was transferred to the Dover-Zeebrugge service for a period of six months in order that the company could maintain their daily schedules across the Dover Strait and Southern North Sea. During this period the *Stena Nordica* was chartered to operate the

*Top: The stretched **Gaelic Ferry** alongside at Felixstowe. (Ambrose Greenway)*

*Above: The **Viking Viscount** creeps up the berth at Zeebrugge in December 1984, having passed the **Norwind** on the Leopold II Dam. (John Hendy)*

*Right: The **Viking II** swings off the berth at Zeebrugge on her arrival from Felixstowe. (Ferry Publications Library)*

*The sisters **Viking Viscount** (foreground) and **Viking Voyager** pass each other in the southern North Sea. (FotoFlite)*

Felixstowe-Zeebrugge link.

March 1978 saw the start of a new and ultimately unsuccessful passenger service between Felixstowe and Rotterdam (Europort) using the former Thoresen ship *Viking III*. With a sailing leaving the Dutch port at 23.59 and an early arrival at Felixstowe at 07.00, the service failed to capture the public's imagination and closed in the following year. The *Viking Victory* (ex *Viking I*) from Portsmouth had taken over the route in October 1978.

Under the new company's management, the port increased its container handling capacity and by 1980 it had grown to become the UK's busiest container port. The management of the port was continued by P&O after 1986. Traffic continued to

grow until such time that the *Cerdic Ferry* became capacity constrained and she was withdrawn from service in 1981. The company immediately chartered the large 'Searunner' class *Stena Transporter* and her sister *Merzario Hispania* (6,455 gross tons) which, in the best Atlantic Steam tradition, they renamed *Baltic Ferry* and *Nordic Ferry*.

FALKLANDS TASK FORCE

When in early April 1982, Argentine forces had invaded the Falkland Islands, a task force was hastily assembled and sailed to the South Atlantic to repatriate the archipelago. Among the Ships Taken Up From Trade (STUFT) were the *Baltic Ferry* and the *Nordic Ferry* along with the 'Europic'

Top: The **Nordic Ferry** (ex **Merzario Hispania**) was one of four sister ships eventually purchased for services from Felixstowe and with her sister ship **Baltic Ferry** (ex **Stena Transporter**) served with distinction during the Falklands conflict. (FotoFlite)

Above: In 1985-86 the South Korean-built **Baltic Ferry** and **Nordic Ferry** were converted for passenger use on the Felixstowe-Zeebrugge link and in 1992 were renamed **Pride of Suffolk** and **Pride of Flanders**. (Ferry Publications Library)

Right: The **Nordic Ferry** awaits departure from Felixstowe for Europort while the **Viking Viscount** arrives from Zeebrugge. (Ferry Publications Library)

which was at that time serving from Southampton. The *Baltic Ferry* was equipped with a helipad and carried three army helicopters, 105 troops, and 1,874 tons of stores and ammunition to Ajax Bay on 1st June while the *Nordic Ferry* was also equipped with a helipad and carried troops, stores, and ammunition to the Falklands on 29th May. She returned to the UK on 29th July 1982 and was refitted to return her to civilian service on 25th August 1982. During the period of the 'Baltic' and 'Nordic's' absence, the company was fortunate to be able to charter their 'Searunner' class sisters *Hellas* and *Syria* for the duration of the conflict.

Whereas the freighters that had served in the Falklands returned safely to service, disaster was to befall another which had been switched to Felixstowe to cover for winter refits. On the night of 19th December 1982, some 2.5 miles off Harwich, the *European Gateway* and Sealink's chartered train ferry *Speedlink Vanguard* were involved in a collision which opened a 20 ft gash along the 'Gateway's' hull. In the heavy North Sea swell, the vessel was plunged into darkness and took on a 45 degree list inside three minutes. Within half an hour, she had rolled over onto her starboard side and sunk on a shallow sandbank with the loss of six lives. Fortunately 65 passengers and crew were saved.

The vessel was raised by Dutch salvage experts on the following 26th February after which she was sold on to Greek owners and the *Europic Ferry* was brought back to deputise.

ALL CHANGE

During October 1985, Townsend Thoresen announced plans for a major redevelopment of its Felixstowe, Cairnryan and Portsmouth operations. Unfortunately for Felixstowe, the twin 'Super Vikings' *Viking Viscount* and *Viking Voyager* were to be transferred to the Portsmouth-Cherbourg link in May 1986 while the Europort freighters *Baltic Ferry* and *Nordic Ferry* would be converted to passenger and freight ships for the Zeebrugge route in their place. Whereas the new Zeebrugge ships offered a 30 per cent increase in freight (to 160 units per sailing), crossings were reduced from three to two a day and passenger capacity dropped from 1,200 to just 650 per ship – a firm indication of the reluctance of motorists to use Felixstowe and now with reduced on-board facilities, the future of all

Top: The **Doric Ferry** *was renamed* **European Tideway** *in 1992. (Ferry Publications Library)*

Above: The **Doric Ferry** *and* **Nordic Ferry** *at Felixstowe prior to renaming in 1992. (Ferry Publications Library)*

passenger sailings from the Suffolk port appeared to be uncertain.

The ships each underwent a £5 million refit during which passenger modules were placed on the open vehicle deck forward of their bridges. As such, they always looked rather odd in their new configuration but did at least solve a pressing problem although the new cabins appeared uncomfortably small. The South Korean built sisters *Hellas* and *Syria* were again chartered for the Europort link and renamed *Doric Ferry* and *Cerdic Ferry* before they were eventually purchased in 1994.

Following the P&O Group's takeover of the ailing European Ferries Group in December 1986, it was very much business as usual for the Suffolk port although the formation of P&O European Ferries in the following October brought about a change of livery for the local fleet.

In 1992 a general renaming policy took place within the fleet so that the former ASN names ending in 'ic' were lost in preference to P&O's 'Pride of' prefixes for passenger ships and 'European' prefixes for freighters. The new names were as follows:

Townsend Thoresen name	P&O name
Baltic Ferry	*Pride of Suffolk*
Nordic Ferry	*Pride of Flanders*
Cerdic Ferry	*European Freeway*
Doric Ferry	*European Tideway*

During 1991, the P&O Group sold the Felixstowe Dock & Railway Company to Hong Kong based Hutchison Whampoa but continued to trade from the port in exactly the same manner as before.

The closure of the nearby Ipswich-Europort service in April 1995 brought welcome extra traffic to the Felixstowe route to the Netherlands. A brief move of the *European Endeavour* from Dover and the charter of the Norwegian vessel *Arcade Falcon* (9,944 gross tons) meant a sailing every six hours in tandem with the resident freighters *European Freeway* and *European Tideway*. After the Dover ship had returned to Kent in June, the 75-trailer *Arcade Eagle* was chartered to run with her sister.

Great efforts were made by local management to promote the Zeebrugge passenger route and, in a move to improve traffic figures, it was even remarketed as the 'Clipper Line' in 1994. Sadly all this hard work came to nothing and it was decided to close the passenger link on 22nd October 1995, the company claiming that this was mainly due to the run down of the British Army in Germany.

Following this, both the passenger ships had their modules removed at Harland & Wolff, Belfast, to allow them to carry more freight although their names were not changed. They were duly moved to operate with their sisters on the Europort link whilst chartered tonnage in the form of the 70-trailer sisters *Gabrielle Wehr* and *Thomas Wehr* (sub-chartered from P&O at Portsmouth) kept the Zeebrugge link operational. In October 1999 they were replaced by the 75-trailer Swedish vessels *Radona* and *Sapphire* which were not only faster on passage but also had the advantage of internal ramps rather than lifts. Consequently, turn round times were bettered and they proved to be easier to load and unload.

P&O NORTH SEA FERRIES AND SALE

During September 1996, the P&O Group purchased a 50 per cent share of their partners on their North Sea Ferries links from Hull, Royal Nedlloyd, for £25.5 million. With effect from New Year's Day 1997, both North Sea Ferries and P&O European Ferries (Felixstowe) Ltd would in future trade as P&O North Sea Ferries. Local management was duly switched to Hull but profits on the twin routes continued to benefit from the closure of the Ipswich operation with a 21 per cent increase in freight over the previous year.

The arrival of the *Pride of Rotterdam* at Hull in April 2001 displaced the super-freighter *Norbank* which after a brief visit to Felixstowe returned to support the new cruise-ferry on 19th June. She was back at the Suffolk port during mid-August replacing the *Pride of Suffolk* which sailed to Hull prior to transfer to the Irish Sea (where she was named *European Diplomat*) and the 'Tideway' which was laid up. However, a further change of plan saw the twin super-freighters transferred to the Irish Sea in the New Year 2002 and the retrieval of the 'Tideway' from lay-up.

In 2002, in a major overhaul of its North Sea operations and

The **Pride of Flanders** (ex **Nordic Ferry**) in her passenger mode and on service to Zeebrugge. (FotoFlite)

as part of a larger fleet reshuffle involving Stena Line, P&O sold both its Felixstowe routes to the Swedish company and also announced the closure of the Dover-Zeebrugge service. At the same time P&O took over Stena Line's 40 per cent share of its stake in the Dover-Calais route and in a move to become a fitter, leaner company during a time of extremely difficult trading conditions, duly shed a number of its periphery services in order that it could in future concentrate on its core routes. In a statement the company said that the decision reflected the inability of the routes "to achieve an adequate return, despite the best efforts of our management". During the previous year, the P&O ferry division had lost £1 million and it was stated that the impact of the foot and mouth epidemic had wiped £13 million from company profits.

After 28 years, the 91-mile link to Zeebrugge duly closed

without ceremony on 6th July 2002 after which the twin charter ships were returned to their owners. On the 119-mile crossing to Europort, the transfer to Stena Line was seamless and under new ownership, the service continued to run from Felixstowe for a further six weeks. The Suffolk connection was finally severed on 14th September with neighbouring Harwich becoming the UK terminal on the following day.

After being handed back to Stena Line, the *European Freeway* was renamed *Freeway* and then *Stena Partner* in the following January. Meanwhile the *European Tideway* became the *Ideway* and then finally the *Stena Transfer*. In 2010, they were sold for scrapping in China. Meanwhile, the *Pride of Flanders* became the *Stena Transporter* and was resold for further work in the Mediterranean during 2011.

TILBURY-ZEEBRUGGE

The most recent route operated by P&O Ferries was founded for the benefit of the growing unaccompanied freight market between the Thames and the Continent. This received a major boost on 16th July 2007 with the introduction of a dedicated ro-ro service linking Tilbury with Zeebrugge, a distance of 123 miles. With its close proximity to the M25 London Orbital Motorway, Tilbury was ideally sited for such trade and P&O were quick to exploit an opportunity.

P&O Ferries initially chartered the small and elderly, red-hulled ferry *Calibur* (ex *Seaspeed Dana*), the vessel having been made available by the recent failure of the Ferryways service from the Humber to Ostend. The Maltese-flag ferry was capable of accommodating 95 trailers and early indications showed that with a second freighter in service during the autumn, as many as 100,000 units would be shipped during the first year alone. The 31-year-old ferry found it difficult to maintain the advertised schedules and so an awkward 25-hour rolling schedule of departures was introduced during the week.

The second vessel duly arrived on 17th September in the form of the 90-trailer capacity *Hoburgen*. Dating from 1986, the vessel was one of eight identical Romanian-built sisters, many of which were familiar with the Thames through previous charters to the erstwhile Dart Line and with Cobelfret. The *Calibur* was switched to the Hull-Zeebrugge service during November 2007 returning to Tilbury in the following January. During her period of absence, her roster was taken by the larger and faster *Global Carrier*.

P&O's own *Norcape* (ex *Tipperary*) eventually superseded the *Calibur* in May 2008. The Japanese-built ship hailed from 1979 although during 1988 she had enjoyed a charter to North Sea Ferries on their Ipswich-Europort and Hull-Zeebrugge links. With capacity for 125 x 12-metre trailers, she remained on the link for six months until replaced in October.

During January 2008, the *European Endeavour* was briefly moved from Dover to cover the refit period. With the route becoming increasingly popular with road hauliers and growing demand for both accompanied and unaccompanied freight, a well-tried pair of ships was now required. With the first phase of the expansion of the Tilbury ro-ro terminal completed, in early October 2008 came the larger and faster *Norking* (1990), which was built in Rauma (Finland) for Bore Line and was originally the *Bore King*. The following year she was taken on long-term charter by North Sea Ferries and placed on their Middlesbrough-Zeebrugge service after which she received the North Sea Ferries 'Nor' prefix. The introduction of the *Norking* allowed P&O to maintain a tighter fixed schedule on the link and, with a capacity for 145 freight units, it was only a matter of time before she was joined by her sister ship. The *Norqueen* (ex *Bore Queen*) shadowed the *Norking*'s career and both had been stretched by 28.8 metres during 1996. On 26th October 2009, she followed her sister onto the Tilbury-Zeebrugge link at which time the *Norcape* went to lay up at Hull.

After a 20-year career with P&O, the *Norking* was returned to her owners Bore Line on 14th September 2011 when she was replaced by the impressive 210-trailer *Norstream* from the Middlesbrough Teesport-Zeebrugge route. The *Norking* was promptly sold to Salamis Lines of Greece and renamed *Alios*.

MIDDLESBROUGH (TEESPORT)-ZEEBRUGGE & EUROPORT

A new freight service linking Middlesbrough and Zeebrugge was opened on 8th May 1988. The vessel chartered to start the new service was the French-flag *Aquila*, dating from 1973 and which was required to operate three round sailings each week. Unfortunately she proved less than satisfactory and so the German *Wesertal* was acquired later in the year, completing the 268-mile journey in 18 hours and offering 760 lane metres of freight with accommodation for 12 drivers.

The following year, NSF introduced the chartered Cypriot-registered *Beaverdale* (1,597 gross tons) thereby allowing nightly sailings from both ports excepting Saturdays. Traffic soon grew and in 1992 the *Beaverdale* was replaced by the German ro-ro ship *Thomas Wehr*. However, this was only a temporary solution to the route's capacity problems and in November the Finnish-flag *Bore King* and *Bore Queen* came on station. At 6,850 gross tons, the sisters represented a major expansion and won popular appeal by virtue of their ease of loading, on-board facilities and by removing 90 minutes from the crossing time. So popular did the sisters become that between October 1995 and January 1996, they were each stretched by 28.8 metres and also re-engined during an eight-week period at Landskrona in Sweden. The new engines gave the ships some 30 per cent more power and a speed of 19 knots. A second bow-thrust unit was added at the same time in order to improve manoeuvrability in port. Capacity rose from 114 to 155 x 12-metre units and turn round times were also enhanced by the installation of internal ramps which replaced the previous lift system between decks. During their absence, their rosters were covered by the *Norcove* (ex *Cupria*).

SECOND LINK

A further route to Europort was opened on 6th March 1995 using the 10,279 gross tons Swedish ro-ro vessel *Cupria* with her capacity for 95 x 12-metre trailers. She had come to the route after a brief service on the Hull-Europort route where she had covered for the *Norsun* which had been marooned in a Rotterdam dry dock following an industrial dispute. Early indications were that the route would succeed and within six weeks, on 22nd April, a further vessel, the new 80-trailer *Bravo* (8,407 gross tons), was brought in to offer a daily service in each direction. The vessels were duly renamed *Norcove* and *Norcliff* but the charter of the latter was not renewed after April 1996 as there was then not enough traffic on offer to justify a two-ship operation. However, the small *Roseanne* was taken on short-term charter in June 1997 and she was followed by the larger *Tidero Star* (9,686 gross tons) on 12th August.

The Zeebrugge route was strengthened in July and November 1999 when the new Rauma-built 'trailerships' *Norsky* and *Norstream* (19,992 gross tons) were taken on an eight-year charter from Bore Line carrying as many as 210 x 12-metre freight units which represented a 35 per cent increase in capacity. Their introduction allowed the smaller chartered *Norking* and *Norqueen* (145 x 12-metre units) to be transferred to the Europort link in August in place of the *Norcove* (ex *Cupria*) and the *Tidero Star* which was retained until the arrival of the second new ship. She then moved to

Top: P&O Ferrymasters' **Elk** *maintained the Teesport-Gothenburg link for 23 years until sold out of service in 2000.*

Above: The **Norcape** *(ex* **Tipperary***, ex* **Puma***) saw service on all of P&O's North Sea freight routes before being transferred to the Irish Sea sector. (Gordon Hislip)*

Hull to replace the *Norcape* which moved to Felixstowe to cover dry dockings.

During March 2008, P&O acquired the 30-year-old freighter *European Trader* (4,928 gross tons, ex *Dana Maxima*). During her lengthy career, the ship had been used on a variety of North Sea routes and in 1995 had been lengthened by 35 metres.

Following her purchase she was initially used on the Hull-Europort link and later during refit periods but early in October 2008 was switched to the Teesport-Europort route to operate with the *Norqueen* after the *Norking* had been switched to the Thames service. She remained on the route until January 2011 when she was transferred to the Zeebrugge link before finishing on 19th April and sailing to Turkish breakers on 25th May 2012.

During spring 2011, the Latvian-registered *Tor Baltica* was on charter maintaining the Zeebrugge service. This vessel was none other than the former *Elk* of the P&O Ferrymasters Middlesbrough-Gothenburg route.

On 11th September 2011 the company took the new highly efficient Flensburg-built *Bore Song* on 37-month time charter. Representing the latest generation of ro-ro vessels, she replaced the *Norstream* which was duly cascaded to the Tilbury-Zeebrugge link. The *Bore Song* offers 2,863 lane metres of freight and a Main Deck height of 7.4 metres thereby allowing the double stacking of containers. With the *Bore Song* maintaining the Zeebrugge link and the *Norsky* transferred to the Europort service, the capacity increase demonstrated P&O's willingness to respond to current and future traffic demands on the twin routes.

IPSWICH-EUROPORT

A subsidiary 120-mile route linking Ipswich with Europort was commenced in March 1977 and operated by North Sea Ferries in conjunction with P&O Ferrymasters. The initial ship to be chartered was an unusual choice in the Stena Line passenger ferry *Stena Normandica* which operated carrying just 12 drivers and with the majority of her capacious accommodation closed down. Six round sailings each week were initially offered until in the following March, the *Norsky* entered service on a bareboat charter. The South Korean

vessel was one of 11 similar 'Searunner' class ro-ro ships built at Ulsan, this particular ship having had stabilisers fitted in addition to a buoyancy tank between her screws to make her more suitable for operation in the shallow River Orwell. Services were from the West Bank Terminal at Ipswich and continued until the *Norsky*'s charter terminated at the end of 1980.

She was duly replaced by the 1979-built *Ibex* (6,310 gross tons) which was transferred from Pandoro's Irish Sea services. Renamed *Norsea* for her new role with NSF, in October 1986 the name was required by the new super-ferry at Hull after which she was also renamed *Norsky*. Earlier in the same year had also seen the introduction of a second ship on 6th January. The German-registered *Argo* (94 trailers) started a three-year charter and allowed up to 11 sailings to be advertised each week. At the conclusion of her charter, in 1989, the Irish Sea freighter *Tipperary* was acquired and renamed *Norcape*. A sister ship of the *Norsky*, the operation of the twins provided a much-need balance to the Ipswich route.

Due to a complex series of circumstances, the route was unfortunately closed on 23rd April 1995 after P&O Ferrymasters had opted to transfer their *Norsky* to the Pandoro route between Liverpool and Dublin and re-direct their traffic via Felixstowe, just downstream from Ipswich. NSF was left with a problem as shippers had come to expect a two-ship service and it was not possible to find a suitable replacement for the absent *Norsky*. The draught and length limitations of the narrow River Orwell meant that only a limited number of vessels could be employed on the route and when no suitable tonnage was available to replace her, it was sadly concluded that the service was no longer viable. The *Norcape* was duly transferred to the Hull-Zeebrugge link where her speed and greater capacity greatly assisted the *Merchant Victor* which had been struggling by herself for six months.

P&O FERRYMASTERS MIDDLESBROUGH-GOTHENBURG/ HELSINGBORG

P&O Ferrymasters is one of the leading European providers of tailor-made transportation and logistics services. The company began operations, as Ferrymasters, in Lancashire

*Sailing down the Thames from Tilbury to Zeebrugge, the **Norstream** originally operated to the Belgian port from Middlesbrough. (John Bryant)*

during 1953 and today has 25 operational bases spread across the Continent.

The *Elk* was one of a series of 11 ro-ro freighters of the 'Searunner' class built in the late 1970s in South Korea, many of which had throughout their long careers, associations with UK ports (e.g. the four ro-ro ships latterly operated by P&O North Sea Ferries from Felixstowe to Europort and Zeebrugge).

Constructed by Hyundai Heavy Industries at Ulsan, the *Elk* was duly delivered to Stena Line and immediately chartered to P&O Ferrymasters for their Middlesbrough-Gothenburg link. She was sold to P&O the following year and in 1981 was used on the Rotterdam-Ipswich link before in May 1982 joining her sisters *Nordic Ferry* and *Baltic Ferry* on charter to the Ministry of Defence as part of the Falklands Task Force. On her return from hostilities she again took up the Tees-Sweden link and four years later was lengthened at Dunkirk. Traffic was obviously buoyant on the twice-weekly route.

Various extra ships were brought in to supplement the crossings at different times and summer 1998 saw the Italian-registered *Norse Mersey* (13,500 gross tons) supporting. From the start of New Year 1999, the *Elk* was transferred into the management of P&O North Sea Ferries having previously been part of the P&O Ferries (Irish Sea) division. The chartered vessel was withdrawn from service in April 1999 leaving the *Elk* to continue with her two services a week. After offering passenger voyages on the route for many years which found much favour amongst the limited number of passengers who were aware of them, these were sadly withdrawn after September.

After a faithful service of 23 years, in December 2000 the *Elk* was sold with the assets of P&O Ferrymasters Scandinavia to DFDS Tor Line and renamed *Tor Baltica*.

Chapter 4

Linking the
with Ireland

Due to the complexities and development of the ferry operations from the sixties on the Irish Sea; for ease of understanding of the P&O's development, the history is divided into two sections in this chapter: Firstly, the opening section deals with history of the Atlantic Steam Navigation Company Ltd, which was later acquired by European Ferries (Townsend Thoresen). ASN's operations focused initially on Preston and then Cairnryan and following the takeover of the company, the Cairnryan-Larne service developed as the main passenger service for the Dover-based company between Scotland and Ireland. Following the takeover of Townsend Thoresen by P&O, the passenger and freight operations were merged in the early nineties into the trading company of P&O Irish Sea.

The second part of this chapter looks at the development of Pandoro freight operations from the seventies, which eventually became part of P&O Irish Sea passenger and freight services, with their five routes between the UK and Ireland and Ireland to France.

DEVELOPING THE DRIVE-ON FREIGHT CONCEPT

The founder and major driving force of the Atlantic Steam Navigation Company Ltd, Frank Bustard, was born in Liverpool in 1886. On leaving school at the age of 16, he joined the then White Star Line as the last of the company's office apprentices. By 1934 Frank Bustard was the Passenger Traffic Manager. In the same year, the Government merged Cunard Line with White Star Line when he was asked by the directors of both companies to accept service with the new merged operation, but he declined. Frank Bustard felt that Cunard would be entirely opposed to his ideas for broadening the approach to travel on the Northern Atlantic with cheaper fares.

He opened his own office right opposite the old White Star offices and two years later the Atlantic Steam Navigation Company Limited was formed. Following the formation of the company, he set about negotiating the acquisition of the necessary vessels to operate his new service. At first he was not successful but he pursued his project nevertheless with undaunted determination.

In the meantime Frank Bustard was called up for the Army

*Top: A packed **Empire Cerdic** moves out of the Albert Edward Dock, Preston into the the River Ribble. (Ferry Publications Library)*

*Above: The **Empire Gaelic** arrives at Larne on 10th May 1965 at the opening of the Phoenix Quay. (Ferry Publications Library)*

Reserve. During the War he made friends with Don Smith, of Messrs Smith, Coggins & Company, the leading stevedores in Liverpool for the Government shipments to the Forces overseas. Both Frank Bustard and Don Smith were present at the trials of the Naval LSTs (Landing Ship (Tank)) for discharging military vehicles over their bow ramps onto the sands at New Brighton. They both considered at the time that there surely would be a commercial use for these craft after the war.

Frank Bustard tried to revive his North Atlantic plans after the war but it soon became clear to him that no suitable ships were available and building new tonnage was out of the question. His thoughts then went back to his meeting with Don Smith regarding operating LSTs for commercial use. He opened negotiations for the charter of three LSTs with the Ministry of War Transport, the Admiralty and the War Office. Following protracted talks, he was successful in chartering for three years the three British LSTs, 3519, 3534 and 3512. They were to be named *Empire Baltic*, *Empire Cedric* and *Empire Celtic*, thus perpetuating the names of White Star vessels. The chartered vessels had to be adapted for their new role before entering service.

On 11th September 1946 the first voyage of the Atlantic Steam Navigation Company Ltd (ASN) took place, when the *Empire Baltic* sailed from Tilbury to Rotterdam with a full cargo of 64 vehicles for the Dutch Government. The service was later moved to Antwerp in 1955. In 1948, the original trio of LSTs was joined by a further vessel of similar class, the *Empire Doric*, after the company had convinced commercial operators to support a new service between mainland Britain and Ulster.

ASN had originally wanted to open their new service to Northern Ireland from Liverpool, but there was opposition from other operators at the Mersey port. In the light of this the company decided to establish themselves at Preston, Lancashire. On the other hand the port authorities at Larne were to welcome the new operation. At Larne end-loading facilities were available in the form of a ramp built by the Army during the War. At Preston a new terminal and ramp had to be built.

Following the inaugural sailing on 21st May 1948, the

*The **Bardic Ferry** on sea trials in the Clyde in August 1957.*
(Ferry Publications Library)

BARDIC FERRY

Top: The Second Class Lounge Bar on board the **Bardic Ferry**. *(Ferry Publications Library)*

Above: The well-appointed de luxe cabin on the **Bardic Ferry**. *(Ferry Publications Library)*

Empire Cedric maintained the Northern Ireland service, initially offering two sailings a week. When the Larne service opened, sceptics declared that it would not last more than six months. Trading continued to expand on the Preston-Larne service and in 1950 services were extended from the Lancashire port to include Belfast. A further vessel, the *Empire Gaelic*, joined the ranks of the fleet to open the new service. The Belfast link opened in 1950 and sailings from Preston were soon to be increased to between six and seven a week to either Larne or Belfast.

In April 1954, ASN was taken over by the British Transport Commission (BTC) as part of the Labour Government's policy for nationalisation. Two years later, the Government took over the entire ASN fleet for use in the Mediterranean during the Suez Crisis and it was not until January 1957 that the drive-on services were re-established at the end of the hostilities. During the Suez War the Preston unit-load service was maintained by chartering three British coasters.

NEW PURPOSE-BUILT SHIPS

During 1957, ASN were to acquire their first two purpose-built vessels with the financial backing of the BTC. The new ships were especially designed for the company for the carriage of lorries, trailers, cars and passengers. The first ferry, the *Bardic Ferry*, was launched on 5th March 1957 at William Denny and Brothers at Dumbarton. The design of the new ships was developed from the 11 years of operation of LSTs. The *Bardic Ferry* and her later sister, the *Ionic Ferry*, were designed to take up to 70 vehicles or trailers on the vehicle deck reached by a stern ramp. Accommodation was provided for 55 passengers in two classes. The *Bardic Ferry* made her maiden voyage on 2nd September 1957 between Preston and Larne under the command of Captain Green. The 'Bardic's' sister, the *Ionic Ferry* was launched in May 1958 and entered service from Preston on 10th October allowing the *Bardic Ferry* to be transferred to the Tilbury-Antwerp link.

During late 1959, two new ships were ordered from Ailsa Shipbuilding Company Limited, Troon and were to be of a very similar design and appearance to the 'Bardic' and 'Ionic', but were to be slightly larger than the original twins. These two new vessels could accommodate about 50 lorries and trailers on the main deck with a headroom of 4.4 metres. The new ships were built as one-class ships with accommodation for 35 passengers in two-berth cabins-de-luxe on the Promenade Deck and two- and four-berth cabins on the Upper Deck. The first of the new twin ferries the *Cerdic Ferry*, was launched on 16th February 1961 and entered commercial service during November the same year, initially operating one trip a week to Rotterdam and two sailings to Antwerp. On the entry into service of the *Cerdic Ferry*, the *Ionic Ferry* was transferred back to the Preston-Northern Ireland services.

During 1962 the British Transport Commission (BTC) was dissolved and ASN's ownership was transferred under the Transport Act of 1962 to the newly formed Transport Holding Company.

With four purpose-built ships in operation, the LSTs were gradually withdrawn from operations. By 1963, only the *Empire Nordic* remained in service on the Preston-Belfast service until she made her last sailing in December 1966.

In October 1963, the Company's fifth purpose-built vessel was launched. The *Gaelic Ferry* was built again as a one-class vessel with accommodation for 28 passengers. On her main cargo deck she could accommodate over 100 trailers or lorries. The *Gaelic Ferry* did not have her own crane on her upper deck like her earlier sisters, as freight traffic was growing at such a rapid rate.

During 1966, the news came that the company was to order its sixth vessel to meet the ever-increasing demand on their links between the UK, Europe and Northern Ireland. The *Europic Ferry* was launched on Tuesday 3rd October 1967. She was not only the largest and fastest vessel ever built for the company but was the last ASN ship to be ordered. Following her launch at Swan Hunter (Shipbuilders) Limited, Wallsend, the *Europic Ferry* was delivered to her owners on 29th December 1967, sadly some four months late. With the arrival of the *Europic Ferry* at Felixstowe, the 'Cerdic's' sister *Doric Ferry* was then transferred to the Preston-Belfast service in November 1968.

With a bigger fleet by the sixties and more services to maintain, ASN had to look to other companies for charter vessels during the overhaul periods of the ships each year. ASN chose to charter the smart-looking 'Viking' ferries from

*Top: The **Ionic Ferry** pictured shortly after her launch in May 1958. She replaced the 'Bardic' on the Northern Ireland services. (Ferry Publications Library)*

*Above: The **Ionic Ferry** arriving at Larne harbour from Preston in 1961. (Ferry Publications Library)*

*Top: The **Free Enterprise III** arriving at Cairnryan from Larne in July 1974. (Paul Clegg Collection)*

*Above: The distinctive livery of ASN was to disappear during 1976 in favour of the Townsend Thoresen orange hull. The **Doric Ferry** is seen here arriving at Larne in the new livery. (Ferry Publications Library)*

Thoresen Car Ferries at Southampton to maintain operations. The charter period of the Thoresen ships usually took place between January and March each year when they were not required on the French services.

ENTER TOWNSEND THORESEN

Under the Transport Act of 1968, the ownership of ASN was transferred once again, this time to be a subsidiary of the newly formed National Freight Corporation. A year later, plans were made to sell ASN to private enterprise at the same time as the company began to implement plans for the repair of its Cairnryan Pier, on the South West Coast of Scotland, following the company purchasing it in the sixties for £60,000. The pier was to be repaired for a new passenger and freight service to Larne. The development of Cairnryan was eventually to see the closure of Preston, in the light of labour problems at the port and difficult navigation of the River Ribble. As part of the Conservative Government's policy of transferring back into private enterprise those nationalised companies which were viable, ASN and its subsidiaries, the Transport Ferry Service (Nederland) NV and Frank Bustard and Sons Limited became part of the European Ferries Group on 18th November 1971. European Ferries, better known as Townsend Thoresen, acquired the goodwill of four routes, seven ferries and three terminals for £5.5 million. The sale of the ASN Group took place in the 25th year of the company's operations.

Following the takeover of ASN operations by the European Ferries Group, the distinctive fleet of 'The Transport Ferry Service' was to remain intact for a further couple of years. Following the takeover, the new management quickly endorsed the decision to move from Preston to Cairnryan. The original purpose-built ferry the *Ionic Ferry* was chosen to open the new service as from 1973. She was sent for refit, following the Preston-Larne service closing on 24th March 1973, and her passenger certificate was increased from 55 to 219 passengers. On Monday, 10th July 1973, the *Ionic Ferry* opened the new service under the command of Captain W. Close. Initially, the *Ionic Ferry* sailed twice a day from Larne at 09.00 and 16.00 with sailings from Scotland at 12.30 and 19.30.

Following the closure of the Preston-Larne service, the Preston-Belfast link was increased to a daily service each way with the *Bardic Ferry* and *Doric Ferry*. The Belfast route was to be abandoned a year later on Saturday 29th July 1974 in favour of the now well-established Larne-Cairnryan service.

In spring 1974, the news came from Dover that *Free Enterprise III* would be transferred to the Irish service as from 1st July. The new ship for the link would provide drive-on/drive-off facilities and would join the *Ionic Ferry* for the summer. With a capacity for 250 cars and 1,200 passengers in one class, the *Free Enterprise III* was to make a sudden and dramatic change to the link. The summer schedules for the Larne service in 1975 initially did not make provision for a passenger car ferry as in the previous year but with a lull in the strife in Northern Ireland, the *Free Enterprise I* was transferred to the link from Dover for the summer period only. The next year *Free Enterprise IV* was switched from Dover to the route as from May 1976. She was to become a great success and firm favourite on the link for the next ten years. During the next couple of years the *Doric Ferry* and *Cerdic Ferry* were to be the operating partners with the *Free Enterprise IV* on the Ulster service.

During March 1980, the *European Gateway* was transferred from Felixstowe to cover the dry-docking period of *Free Enterprise IV* and the *Doric Ferry* until June. A new double-deck linkspan was completed at Cairnryan during 1980, thereby allowing double-deck loading at both the Scottish port and Larne. In September 1980, the *European Gateway* was sent for lengthening by 15.7 metres to increase her freight capacity and add additional passenger areas. A year later the *Cerdic Ferry* and *Doric Ferry* were withdrawn from service and offered for sale.

The *European Gateway* returned to the Ulster link again in 1981, following her lengthening, for nearly a year with the *Free Enterprise IV*. On the night of Sunday 19th December, the *European Gateway* was lost off Felixstowe in a collision with the *Speedlink Vanguard*. The *Europic Ferry* at the Suffolk port took her place. Meanwhile, the *Gaelic Ferry* was transferred to the Northern Ireland link until March 1983, when she was replaced by the *Europic Ferry*.

FLEET CHANGES

During 1985, European Ferries decided upon a major

Top: The **European Gateway** *arriving at Cairnryan during her first season on the Ulster link. (Ferry Publications Library)*

Above: In 1976 the **Free Enterprise IV** *was switched from Dover to the North Channel service. She is seen here arriving at the Scottish port during her first season. (Ferry Publications Library/P&O Library)*

redevelopment of their fleet at Portsmouth, Felixstowe, Larne and Dover. At Cairnryan, *Free Enterprise IV* was transferred back to Dover to operate with the *Free Enterprise V* on the Boulogne route; her place was taken by the former P&O Ferries vessel *Dragon* from Portsmouth. The *Free Enterprise IV* sailed south on 10th July 1986 following the arrival of the *Ionic Ferry* (ex *Dragon*) after a month's refit at Glasgow. The cabins and passenger areas situated aft on the *Ionic Ferry* were removed during her refit to enable her top deck area at the stern to be used for the carriage of high-sided vehicles. The *Ionic Ferry*, with her operating partner the *Europic Ferry*, then settled down into a regular pattern of sailings on the link.

The 'Europic' and 'Ionic' partnership lasted until 1992 when the stretched Dover-Zeebrugge twins *Pride of Sandwich* (ex *Free Enterprise VI*) and *Pride of Walmer* (ex *Free Enterprise VII*) were replaced in the Dover Strait and made available for the North Channel, becoming the *Pride of Ailsa* and *Pride of Rathlin*. Capacity was boosted on the shortest route to Ireland and the last ASN ship, the *Europic Ferry*, was downgraded to freight-only purposes and was renamed *European Freighter*.

In June 1996, P&O European Ferries chartered the revolutionary £20 million monohull fast craft, *Jetliner*. The 600 passengers, 160-car vessel was able to cross the North Channel in just one hour and offered six sailings a day. Her arrival saw the withdrawal of the *Pride of Ailsa*, which was sold to Egypt, while former Dover ro-ro vessels *European Endeavour* and *European Trader* joined the route to boost freight capacity in September 1995 and February 1996.

NEW TONNAGE

During January 1999, P&O European Ferries announced details of the construction of a new 21,000 gross ton passenger and freight vessel from Mitsubishi Heavy Industries of Japan for delivery in June 2000. The new ship would operate between Larne and Cairnryan with a speed of 23 knots, reducing the conventional ferry time by a quarter to just 105 minutes, and would be complemented at the time by the 60-

*This aerial view shows the **Europic Ferry** with her wealth of freight space on her upper deck, which was ideal for the North Channel route with special high-sided freight lorries. (Ferry Publications Library)*

Top: The **Free Enterpise IV** *leaves Larne on her evening sailing to Scotland.* *(Miles Cowsill)*

Above: The **Ionic Ferry** *(ex **Dragon**) arrives at Cairnryan during her first season following her transfer from the English Channel. (Miles Cowsill)*

Right: The **Europic Ferry** *arrives at Larne in August 1987 with a blue funnel pending the P&O house flag being adopted. (Miles Cowsill)*

Above left: The **Europic Ferry** *leaves Larne in full P&O livery following the takeover of the company and the demise of the Townsend Thoresen name. (Miles Cowsill)*

Above right: The funnel of the **Europic Ferry** *sporting the P&O house flag. (Miles Cowsill)*

Below: The **Ionic Ferry** *swings off the berth at Larne on her afternoon sailing from Scotland. (Miles Cowsill)*

*The former Dover-based freight vessel **European Endeavour** was switched to the North Channel to offer additional capacity in 2005. (Miles Cowsill)*

minute fast ferry service operated by the *Jetliner*. She would be constructed with twin decks with drive-through bow and stern loading and would be able to handle a mix of passengers and freight, with space for 375 cars or 107 commercial vehicles. Ultimately, she would replace the *Pride of Rathlin*, which would be disposed of. Commenting on the announcement, Graeme Dunlop, Chairman of P&O Ferries, said, "Our new ferry will offer passengers the very latest facilities at the same time as giving them an even faster crossing. It will further strengthen P&O's position as one of the leading operators on the Irish Sea."

On 20th March 2000, the *European Causeway* was launched in Japan. Following her launch, the remaining superstructure and fitting-out of the ship was completed in the yard prior to her final delivery voyage. The *European Causeway* entered commercial service in August 2000, which allowed the *Pride of Rathlin* to be withdrawn and sold. The former Dover ship made her last commercial sailing on 11th September 2000 (21.30 ex Larne). The new purpose-built ship for the route made an immediate impact on the Larne-Cairnryan service. P&O were given an option by the Japanese yard at the time of the order for the *European Causeway* for a third vessel; and P&O took the option for a second ship to be built to operate with the *European Causeway* on the North Channel in late 2000. The *European Highlander* was delivered by her Japanese builders to P&O in 2002 and entered commercial service in the July in tandem with her identical sister the *European Causeway*. The two sisters have successfully operated P&O's North Channel operation with very little interruption or delays since their introduction.

In April 2000, the *Jetliner* was replaced by the *Superstar Express* from Portsmouth. Following the reorganisation of P&O Ferries in 2005, she was in turn replaced by the *Express*, which had been operating on the English Channel at Portsmouth. For the last seven years she has maintained the seasonal fast ferry service between Larne and Cairnryan and Larne and Troon, plus charter work for Steam Packet during TT Races in June.

In 2011, P&O's rivals on the North Channel, Stena Line, moved their Loch Ryan port from Stranraer to the newly established port just north of P&O's operations at Cairnryan.

*Top: This view shows the jumboised former **Free Enterpise VII** leaving Larne as the **Pride of Rathlin** following her transfer to the North Channel. (Miles Cowsill)*

*Above: The Bermudian-registered **Jetliner** leaves Cairnryan during her first season on the North Channel. (Miles Cowsill)*

*Top: The **European Trader** arriving at Larne harbour with the distinctive Ballylumford Power Station behind her. (Miles Cowsill)*

*Above: The **Pride of Ailsa** at her berth at Larne pending her evening sailing to Scotland. (Miles Cowsill)*

*Right: The **Pride of Rathlin** leaves Loch Ryan during her last season on the route. (Miles Cowsill)*

Above left: The **European Causeway**, *built in Japan, brought much-needed new tonnage to P&O's North Channel service. (Miles Cowsill)*

Above right: The **Express** *was introduced on the North Channel in April 2009. She is seen here arriving at Larne in August 2010. (Miles Cowsill)*

Left: The **European Highlander** *inward bound from Larne with Ailsa Craig behind her. (Miles Cowsill)*

Above: A rare view of both the **European Highlander** *and* **European Causeway** *together at Larne. (Miles Cowsill)*

MAX. CLEARANCE 5.2M
MAX. CLEARANCE 5.2M
NO
SMOKING
EUROPEAN HIGHLANDER
NASSAU
P&O

The Swedish company introduced new tonnage on their service from Scotland to Ireland with their move from Stranraer. Today, P&O Irish Sea operate two modern purpose-built ships on their service on the North Channel and they are a far cry from the operation originally established by the Atlantic Steam Navigation Company with the *Ionic Ferry*.

PANDORO

The long-established shipping names Coast Lines (who were at this time 25 per cent shareholders in North Sea Ferries), its subsidiary the Belfast Steamship Company (operating the overnight Liverpool-Belfast link with the car ferries *Ulster Prince* and *Ulster Queen*) and Burns & Laird (operators of the *Lion* on the daylight Ardrossan-Belfast route) disappeared when they were acquired by P&O in 1971. Seeking to increase its road haulage and freight interests these three companies gave an opening to expand and dominate the Irish Sea ferry operations in the early seventies, with their only rivals at the time being Townsend Thoresen (Cairnryan), Sealink (Fishguard, Holyhead, Heysham and Stranraer) and B&I (Liverpool and Swansea). At the same time P&O was able to reorganise its 120 subsidiaries of the three operators into five new divisions.

In 1972, the formation of Ferrymasters (Ireland) Ltd (the parent company of which Coast Lines owned an interest) soon saw a new service operating between Fleetwood and Larne, which commenced operation in June 1973. In the following November the British Transport Docks Board started work on a ro-ro terminal at the Lancashire port and in 1974 P&O purchased the new ro-ro vessels *Bison* and *Buffalo* from Stena Line for £8 million. A further £1.25 million was invested in ro-ro units to be used in connection with the new ships.

Then in December 1974, they founded Pandoro, providing a local transport operation for shippers to Ireland into which Ferrymasters (Ireland) was absorbed. The name was a clever acronym of P AND O RO (i.e. roll on). In addition to the new service to Larne, one of the ships also served Dublin in a new joint venture with the British & Irish Steam Packet Company

*An impressive view of the **European Highlander** arriving at the entrance of Loch Ryan in May 2010. (Miles Cowsill)*

*Top: This view shows the **Ulster Queen** and **Ulster Prince** at Ostend following the demise of the Liverpool-Belfast service. (Miles Cowsill)*

*Above: Pandoro's freight vessel **Buffalo** swings off her berth at the inner docks at Liverpool from Dublin. (Miles Cowsill)*

(B&I). The *Bison* was first in service in February 1975, actually operating her maiden voyage from the Royal Seaforth Dock in Liverpool, while the *Buffalo* followed in March.

The ro-ro trade expanded rapidly at a time when the 'troubles' in Northern Ireland were having a profound effect on the tourist and passenger/car market. Smaller, less profitable services were soon axed as the new Pandoro services went from strength to strength and services to and from Garston, Preston, Warrenpoint, Newry and Londonderry were all closed.

Meanwhile, P&O unveiled their 'new image' in October 1975 when the Belfast Steamship Company and Burns & Laird Lines became P&O Ferries (Irish Sea Services) and the *Ulster Queen* and *Ulster Prince* were duly painted in their pale blue livery. The *Lion* was withdrawn from service at Ardrossan in February 1976, after which she was sent to the Dover Strait to commence a new Normandy Ferries link with Boulogne. The long-established overnight Liverpool-Belfast route was finally withdrawn in November 1981 with losses estimated at £1 million, after which the 'Ulster' boats were laid up for sale in Ostend.

Meanwhile at Liverpool, Pandoro built a ramp and terminal at the North West Alexandra Dock and chartered, then purchased the four-year-old *Union Melbourne* which, after stretching, eventually became the *Puma*. This proved so successful that the *Bison* and *Buffalo* received similar extensions in 1981 and 1988. Further increases in freight saw the *Bison* receive an extra deck in 1995, while three years later the *Buffalo* was given hers.

Further large ro-ro vessels to join the Pandoro fleet were the *Ibex*, which was built in 1979, after which she was chartered to North Sea Ferries between 1980 and 1995, during which time she was named firstly *Norsea* and then *Norsky* before returning to the Liverpool-Dublin service under her original name. She too received an extra deck in 1996.

The *Viking Trader* was built for Stena Line in 1977 but was taken on charter by P&O European Ferries (Portsmouth) Ltd in 1983, at which time she adopted a familiar 'Viking' name. She was transferred to Pandoro in 1989 and eventually renamed the *Leopard* for the Fleetwood-Dublin route.

Following the closure of the Ardrossan-Larne passenger

*The **European Clearway** arrives at Rosslare from Cherbourg during her first season on the route. (Miles Cowsill)*

route in 1976, Pandoro opened a freight service using the *Pointer*; the operation was later moved from Belfast in favour of Larne.

Following the Zeebrugge disaster in March 1987, the Townsend Thoresen name disappeared and a new ferry company was established by P&O for all their ferry operations in the UK, P&O European Ferries. In spite of the changes in the passenger operations, Pandoro continued their freight operations still as a stand-alone operation, as the business model was very different.

In 1993, Pandoro inaugurated a new service linking

Rosslare with Cherbourg using the former Dover-Zeebrugge freighter *European Clearway* in order to operate the link. In January 1996 the vessel was renamed *Panther*. The Ardrossan-Larne link acquired the 1978-built *Merchant Valiant* in 1993, two years later she was purchased and renamed the *Lion*. Meanwhile, the Liverpool-Dublin service was covered by the *Bison* and *Buffalo*, with the *Viking Trader* and *Puma* covering the Fleetwood-Larne.

In 1996 the *Ibex*, which had been built for Pandoro in 1979, was sent to Cammel Laird to have an additional deck added, prior to entering service again on the Liverpool-Dublin service.

*Top: The jumboised **Ibex** leaves Dublin with a full load of Pandoro containers. (Miles Cowsill)*

*Above: This view shows the **Puma** outward bound from Fleetwood and the **Ibex** inward bound to Liverpool. (Ferry Publications Library)*

*Right: The **Bison** unloading at Larne showing her three vehicle decks, two of which could be unloaded simultaneously. (Ferry Publications Library)*

*The **European Mariner** leaves Larne for Ardrossan. The vessel maintained the link until June 2011 and was replaced by the **Norcape**. (Miles Cowsill)*

During late 1997, in preparation for the formation of P&O European Ferries (Irish Sea), the entire Pandoro fleet was renamed with the *Bison* becoming the *European Pioneer*, *Buffalo* renamed *European Leader*, *Ibex* renamed *European Envoy*, *Leopard* renamed *European Navigator*, *Lion* renamed *European Highlander*, *Panther* renamed *European Pathfinder* and the *Puma* becoming *European Seafarer*.

After 30 years from Ardrossan, Pandoro decided to move their freight operations in the autumn of 1999 in favour of Troon as from 2001. P&O claimed at the time that the service had simply outgrown the Ardrossan port facilities. As part of the agreement with Associated British Ports, who owned Troon, a new £4.5 million terminal was constructed for the *European Highlander* (ex *Lion*).

P&O IRISH SEA

In 1999, it was announced that a new £33 million ro-pax had been ordered from Mitsubishi of Japan for the Liverpool-Dublin route for delivery in 2001, which would allow the *European Leader* to transfer to the Fleetwood-Larne route.

Top: Pandoro's **Viking Trader** *is seen here leaving Fleetwood on her morning sailing to Larne. (Miles Cowsill)*

Above: The **European Ambassador** *at Dublin during her first season on the Irish Sea. The vessel was later withdrawn from the Mostyn service and sold by P&O to Stena Line. (Ferry Publications Library)*

The new ship would be able to carry 275 cars or 123 freight units, and would have capacity for 405 passengers.

Early 2000 saw P&O Irish Sea operating three ships on the Liverpool-Dublin route and three freight vessels on the Fleetwood-Larne service. The *European Highlander* continued on the Ardrossan route and the *European Pathfinder* covered the 18-hour route between Rosslare and Cherbourg.

The new Liverpool-Dublin vessel, the *European Ambassador* left her builders in Japan on 13th December, calling at Singapore en route to the Red Sea via the Suez Canal. She arrived in Liverpool on 6th January 2001 under the command of Captain Nicholas Spencer and entered service a week later.

In early 2001, P&O announced further changes to their operations on the Irish Sea. With continued frustration at Liverpool and the lack of river berths, P&O decided to open a new ferry service between Mostyn (North Wales, at the entrance to the River Dee) to Dublin as an alternative service to that of their Liverpool operation using the *European Ambassador* and *European Envoy*. This new port developed in North Wales potentially offered very good links to the A55, linking the M6, but its major drawback was the torturous and tidal restrictions to the harbour, which inevitably was to be its downfall in 2004. The *Celtic Sun* and *Celtic Star* were chartered by P&O to maintain the drop in traffic on the Liverpool service while the accompanied and small passenger market was concentrated on Mostyn. To the benefit of P&O at the time, the new service would allow 1.5 round trips a day out of each ship and a reduced passage between Dublin and Mostyn of five-and-a-half hours. The route opened in November 2001 and was plagued with delays and cancellations due to tidal conditions and weather, and was only to operate for just over two years with the company eventually moving all its operations back to Liverpool.

Following the introduction of the giant *Pride of Rotterdam* and her sister the *Pride of Hull* on the Hull-Europort service, the company decided to transfer the freight vessels *Norbay* and *Norbank* to the Irish Sea to improve their service on the Liverpool-Dublin route. The new ships not only offered improved freight capacity but also would enable P&O Irish Sea to establish and improve their car and passenger facilities on this link. Both ships have operated successfully on the Liverpool-Dublin service since 2002.

In spring 2003 P&O and Stena Line signed a Memorandum of Understanding under which Stena would take over the Liverpool-Dublin and Fleetwood-Larne services from P&O and the now ill-fated Mostyn-Dublin service would be closed. The Fleetwood and Liverpool ships, their crews and personnel would be transferred to the Swedish company. In the event, the plan to take over all the routes did not materialise as originally envisaged. Stena Line took over the Fleetwood-Larne link and the three ships on the service but P&O continued with their Liverpool-Dublin route, following the British Competition Commission failing to allow P&O to sell it to Stena Line. The Mostyn service was closed in April 2004 with the *European Ambassador* being sold to Stena Line for service in the Baltic as the *Stena Nordica*. The *European Envoy* which had partnered the 'Ambassador' was also disposed of, leaving the Liverpool-Dublin service now in the hands of the freight vessels *Norbay* and *Norbank*.

Stena Line made fundamental changes and cost-savings to the Fleetwood-Larne service but in spite of these changes the route closed on 24th December 2010. The route needed substantial investment in new tonnage, which was now 35 years old, but the Achilles' heel was Fleetwood with its tidal restrictions and a very difficult approach passage through a sandbank-lined channel. It is unlikely that Fleetwood will ever see a ferry service again, especially in the light of planned improvements on the Mersey at both Liverpool and Birkenhead.

As part of the restructuring of the P&O Ferries Group, it was decided to withdraw their freight service between Rosslare and Cherbourg in 2005. The *European Diplomat* had been transferred to the Irish/French route some three years earlier in place of the *European Pathfinder* to offer more capacity on the 18-hour service. P&O were successful in selling the operation and the 'Diplomat' transferred to Irish-based company Celtic Link Ferries.

The *European Endeavour* joined the *Norbay* and *Norbank* on the Liverpool-Dublin route in 2011. In a surprise move in December 2011, P&O Irish Sea decided to close their freight service between Larne and Troon following some minor

*Top: The **Norbay** undertaking berthing trials at Troon in 2011. (Gordon Hislip)*

*Above: The **Norbank** arrives at Dublin in the autumn sunshine from Liverpool in October 2010. (Miles Cowsill)*

*The **European Endeavour** leaves Dublin for Liverpool during her first season on the Irish Sea. (Gordon Hislip)*

damage to the *Norcape*, which had replaced the *European Mariner* earlier in the year. There had been hope on both sides of the Irish Sea that the route would be expanded and improved with new tonnage following the *Norbay* undertaking berthing trials earlier in the year at Troon. The fast ferry passenger service continues to operate on a seasonal basis, with P&O now concentrating on the Larne-Cairnryan route as the major freight link into Northern Ireland.

In 2012, P&O Irish Sea operates two passenger and freight services on the Irish Sea and one fast ferry operation between Larne and Cairnryan/Troon. Their Liverpool service is maintained with the *Norbay* and *Norbank* with the *European Endeavour* as back-up ship on the link. The successful and purpose-built *European Causeway* and *European Highlander* maintain the Cairnryan-Larne service on five round sailings each a day on the link. The fast ferry service operated by the *Express* runs normally from March until late October from Larne to Cairnryan and Troon.

The Norbay arrives at Dublin in July 2012. (Miles Cowsill)

Chapter 5

P&O
Scottish Ferries
heritage routes

The crossings to Orkney and Shetland are some of the roughest stretches of water in the British Isles, and can be exceptionally difficult even today during periods of inclement weather, the vessels are unable to sail. It is, however, the proud boast of the various companies, including P&O that during its long existence not one person has been lost in any accident.

Historically, the company traded under the illustrious name of the North of Scotland, Orkney & Shetland Shipping Company Ltd, which was always conveniently abbreviated to the 'North Company'. The old North Company was an amalgamation of a number of small and competing concerns which joined forces in June 1875 offering services from Aberdeen and Leith. The routes offered by the company provided a lifeline to the islands importing coal, timber and other commodities while the export of livestock has always been confined to a short annual period.

The port of Scrabster (two miles from Thurso) was opened during the 1850s and on its arrival in the Caithness town in 1874 the Highland Railway Company sought to operate its own steamer across the Pentland Firth to Stromness. This was accomplished three years later but in 1882 the North Company steamer *St. Olaf* took over its working. Ten years later the first *St. Ola* took up the link and from that time this famous name was always associated with the Pentland Firth crossing.

The services and ships provided a century ago certainly appear very generous when compared with those of today. Three sailings each week were provided from Leith to Orkney and Shetland and all called at Aberdeen en route. The first, known as the west-side boat, sailed via Stromness (Orkney) and Scalloway (Shetland). The second, the 'secondary indirect boat', was via Kirkwall (Orkney) and Lerwick (Shetland) whilst the third (the 'weekend boat') followed the same route with the additional call at the Caithness port of Wick. An additional sailing to Wick and Thurso was called the 'Caithness boat'. Direct sailings linking Aberdeen with Lerwick were instituted in 1891 with the company providing the new *St. Giles* in the following year. Meanwhile, expansion in tourist traffic saw popular cruises to Norway in the *St. Sunniva* and the construction of the company's own hotel at Hillswick

(Shetland) in 1902.

During the period immediately prior to the First World War, the North Company provided the islands with the best service they have ever experienced. Shetland was served five times a week from Leith and Aberdeen, Orkney was served three times, while Caithness received two sailings.

During the 1914-18 war the North Company lost three ships, the *St. Nicholas*, *St. Magnus* and the *St. Margaret* and in order to bide things over, cargo ships were acquired for the first time – the first to be built for the company being the *St. Clement* in 1928.

Competition from the airways first occurred during the mid-1930s and a daily airmail link to Shetland was commenced in 1938. The outbreak of World War II was also to see the North Company in the thick of it. More losses were recorded in the form of the second *St. Sunniva*, *St. Catherine*, *St. Clement* and the *St. Fergus*. Towards the war's end, only two vessels, the *St. Magnus* (Aberdeen-Lerwick) and *St. Rognvald* (Aberdeen-Kirkwall) were available for passenger service, while Leith was served by cargo vessels. Fortunately, the *St. Clair* and the *Earl of Zetland* both returned safely from hostilities, as did the *St. Ninian*, which in view of her age was not returned to service.

The post-war pattern of services was greatly reduced with the Caithness link being made by cargo boat only until its demise in 1956. Gradually, calls to centres in Orkney and Shetland other than to Kirkwall, Stromness and Lerwick (many serviced by 'flitboats' tendering to the steamers which had anchored offshore) were withdrawn, leaving smaller operators and then the respective councils to provide for the transhipment of passengers and cargoes.

In 1961 the company was taken over by Coast Lines Ltd, which, ten years later, was duly absorbed into the P&O Group.

P&O TAKE OVER SERVICES

A new Aberdeen-Lerwick ro-ro ferry order was eventually given to Hall Russell's, Aberdeen in July 1973 for delivery in May 1975. Prior to this order P&O had looked at other vessels in their fleet that might fill the role instead of a new build. Two vessels were considered in late 1974, the *Lion* (Burns & Laird) and the *Norwave* (North Sea Ferries).

Top: The **St Clair** *(III) off the coast of Shetland inward bound to Lerwick. (Lawrence Macduff)*

Above: The **St Clair** *(IV) arriving at Aberdeen from Lerwick in the evening sun. (Lawrence Macduff)*

The new Pentland Firth vessel, the first ro-ro ferry in the fleet, the *St. Ola* (III) was launched at Aberdeen on 24th January 1974 with delivery planned for mid-June. The new *St. Ola* was delayed and made her visit to the Firth of Forth in mid-September for dry-docking and speed trials, and then carried out final trials in Aberdeen Bay on 29th October 1974, later sailing overnight to Stromness. The delays at the shipyard paled into insignificance compared with the delays at Scrabster where the terminal was nowhere near ready. The *St. Ola* lay unused for three months at Stromness before entering service.

Another part of the operations, which had been seeing significant changes, was on the North Isles of Shetland. In the summer of 1970 Zetland County Council received approval to build an inter-island car ferry which would attract a 75 per cent Government Grant. The new ferry would replace the then four vessels and ten purpose-built terminals. The first of Zetland County Council's ferries, the *Fivla*, entered service on 21st May 1973 between Toft (mainland) and Ulsta (Yell), and after a transitional period the *Earl of Zetland* (II) progressively dropped her various calling ports in the North Isles as each new ferry was introduced.

THE NEW GENERATION OF FERRIES

On 26th January 1975 the new *St. Ola* made a circumnavigation of Hoy for crew familiarisation purposes to test all machinery systems. Two days later she made a VIPs crossing to Scrabster and on the following day she finally made her maiden voyage from Stromness to Scrabster. At long last ro-ro had come to fruition, some 11 years after its introduction of such ships in the Western Isles. Internally, the passenger accommodation was confined to the shelter (or upper deck) with a large observation saloon at the fore and a cafeteria/bar at the after end, which was divided down the centre line on an open-plan layout. An entrance foyer and purser's office was amidships. Vehicles had the use of the entire main deck with two wing decks above accessed by lifts and frequently used for livestock.

Meanwhile, during March 1975, the *Lion* was put out to tender for conversion to become the Lerwick ferry, but mounting losses on P&O's long routes (Lisbon, Tangier and

San Sebastian) forced a rethink and in October it was announced that the former *SF Panther* (Southern Ferries of the P&O Group) would be employed instead. She had operated on the Southampton-San Sebastian route until its closure in 1973 and then had been chartered out to Da-No Linje for service in Norway and renamed the *Terje Vigen*.

While the *St. Clair* and the three cargo ships continued as before, the most significant change during that first year of ro-ro was that the Pentland Firth sailings were increased during the summer. The old *St. Ola* had operated extra summer crossings for many years, but these were invariably only as required and traffic patterns generally confined these to the Friday to Monday period while Sunday sailings had become part of the advertised schedule from 1959 (July/August only) onwards. From the beginning of June the *St. Ola* made an extra 15.00 Wednesdays-only crossing from Stromness while on Thursdays five single crossings, commencing at 08.45 from Scrabster, were provided until the end of August. This was mainly to provide a day excursion on Thursdays from the Caithness side but on a number of occasions the Wednesday evening service was employed for charter cruises along the coast or through Scapa Flow and this arrangement continued for a number of years.

At the beginning of October 1975 the North Company title disappeared, the company then traded as P&O Ferries (Orkney & Shetland Services) and the *St. Ola* (III) reappeared from refit in November with P&O pale blue funnels, the first of the visual alterations.

During 1974 preliminary site work had commenced at Aberdeen and Lerwick terminals though the construction phase did not commence until 1976 at Aberdeen and effectively became an extension of the then current Kirkwall freight berths. In the same month all vessels commenced using the new Lerwick facilities at Holmsgarth except for the *St. Clair*, which continued to use the 'mail' berth at Victoria Pier. The Matthew's Quay complex at Aberdeen was finally vacated at the end of October with the *St. Clair* transferring to a temporary berth at Regent's Quay.

In 1975 indications that North Sea oil was to be a major force, particularly in the northern North Sea, resulted in the freight-only ro-ro vessel the *Helga* being purchased by P&O

for management by the North Company. She was renamed the *Rof Beaver* (Rof signifying 'roll-on freighter'), the 'Beaver' being in accord with P&O's then stated policy of using the Burns' fleet animal names for all their ferries. She was Leith-based and with no P&O presence there by then, agents were appointed to look after her. She carried no passengers and the accommodation block was sited right aft. Loading was via the stern ramp and there was a large hold beneath the vehicle deck, which could be conventionally crane-loaded. She was overhauled in Marseilles and made her delivery voyage to Immingham in May, loading for Sullom Voe.

In the islands there was continuous criticism of the 'blue' funnels which became more vociferous at the thought that their cherished 'Saint' names could disappear to be replaced with 'animal' names, but this criticism was allayed when an announcement was made that the *SF Panther* would be renamed the *St. Clair* (IV). With the entry into service of the *St. Clair* on 4th April 1977, Shetland now had full ro-ro services to the outside world. A new lower fares structure from the islands (southbound) was introduced at this time.

Meanwhile, in the same year, P&O decided to open a new route with the *St. Magnus* to Hanstholm in Denmark and Kristiansand in Norway.

DAILY SAILINGS TO SHETLAND

P&O announced plans in 1986 for a second passenger ferry to operate the Aberdeen, Stromness, Lerwick route and additional direct sailings between Aberdeen and Lerwick. The *nf Panther*, formerly of P&O Normandy Ferries' Dover-Boulogne route, was transferred to the company. Built as the *Djursland* for Jydsk Faergesfart of Denmark in 1972, the contract to refit her was awarded to Hall Russell's Aberdeen shipyard. The ship was refitted as an overnight ferry with cabins forward on main and upper passenger decks with restaurant, shop, TV room and bar from aft of mid-ships on the main deck. A self-service restaurant-cum-cinema aft doubled up with reclining seats as the overnight lounge on the upper deck, with more cabins on the port side aft.

The proposed pattern of services was: Monday to Friday evening departures northbound and southbound on Sundays to Thursdays with an additional Saturday midday sailing

*Top: The **St. Ola** (III) operated on the Pentland-Firth service between 1975 and 1992. (Lawrence Macduff)*

*Above: The **St. Sunniva** (ex **nf Panther**) was transferred from the English Channel operations in 1987. (Lawrence Macduff)*

*Right: The **St. Ola** (IV) inward bound from Scrabster during her last season on the link prior to the takeover of the route by NorthLink. (Lawrence Macduff)*

northbound via Orkney. The Friday sailing southbound was to leave Lerwick at midday via Orkney. The *St. Clair* would take the Monday, Wednesday and Friday northbound sailings while the second ship would take the Tuesday, Thursday and Saturday northbound sailings. Sailings on a daily basis to Shetland for passengers had returned. Plans were made to have more mini-cruises for the spring and autumn when the new ship took up the routes but the *St. Clair* undertook most of them.

Mrs Olivia Ford renamed the *nf Panther* the *St. Sunniva* (III) on 27th March 1987. The bridge windows were damaged on the maiden voyage and electrical problems resulted in the ship having to return to Aberdeen. A decision to use stronger glass in all forward windows was made after this voyage!

In 1987 the brochure had a two-page feature on the 150th anniversary of P&O with various events taking place, e.g. the opening of the Bod of Gremista (birthplace of Arthur Anderson, founder of P&O Company), two visits to Leith on consecutive weekends, and an Orkney week promotion was held in Aberdeen.

In January 1989 the company changed the title of their North services once again when P&O Scottish Ferries was adopted. The *St. Clair* made a mini-cruise to Maloy in Norway in spring 1989. Meanwhile, the *St. Sunniva* added mid-week northbound calls each Tuesday at Stromness during the peak season, leaving Aberdeen at midday and Lerwick at midday on Wednesdays. This was linked with a call of about an hour and a half in each direction at Stromness from 1989.

A freight service to Hanstholm (Denmark) was again suggested in 1988 and an additional freight ship was required for this service, so a charter of the *Marino Torre* from Italian owners took place in 1989. She had 50 per cent more freight capacity than the *St. Magnus* so she was eventually bought in as her successor on the indirect service. She was renamed the *St. Rognvald* (IV) which had been built as the *Rhonetal* in 1970 at Lubeck, Germany.

The *St. Magnus* was relieved by the *Juniper* in July 1989 before leaving for a charter on the Southampton to Cherbourg service and being offered for sale. Meanwhile, a second-hand replacement for the *St. Clair* was now planned and £15 million set aside for this purpose. Mr Graeme Dunlop was brought in

to manage this northern outpost for one year while Eric Turner became Chairman of Lloyd's Register of Shipping (Scotland).

THE SECOND GENERATION

The *Tregastel* of Brittany Ferries was purchased in 1991. She was sent to the Lloyd Werft yard at Bremerhaven for conversion work to be done. Meanwhile, the company also purchased the *Eckero* as replacement second-hand tonnage for the Pentland Firth from Eckero Lines of Finland.

The Stromness berth was proving too short for both the *St. Sunniva* (III) and the *St. Rognvald* and so work was put in hand to extend it. While this was being done the *St. Sunniva* served Kirkwall in lieu of Stromness on some sailings and the *St. Rognvald* made extra calls there in addition to her Monday calls.

In 1992, the *Tregastel* joined the fleet as the *St. Clair*. With a gross tonnage of 4,231, she had four passenger decks and two car/vehicle decks and was the largest ship in the fleet. The passenger cabins were mainly on C and D decks; the bar, lounges, restaurant, children's play area, and ship's office on B deck, and the reclining seat lounge on A deck.

A new *St. Ola* entered service on Wednesday 25th March 1992. The main deck had a television lounge forward, ship's office in the foyer, restaurant and shop, while the bar was on the upper deck. She had been built by Jos L. Meyer at Papenburg in 1971 as the *Svea Scarlett*. The *St. Ola*, the fourth ship to carry the name in the company, had a gross tonnage of 4,833, a length of 86.3 metres (283 ft) and a service speed of 15 knots. She was able to carry 500 passengers and up to 110 cars and/or 20 commercial vehicles.

When it was announced that the *Norrona*'s calls at Lerwick were to cease at the end of August 1992, pressure from the local authority, tourist board and others led to a decision to send the *St. Clair* to Bergen in the high season of 1993. The new operation allowed a Friday departure from Aberdeen at 18.00 to Lerwick, then departing from Lerwick during late Saturday morning for Bergen arriving at 22.00 local time with the return sailing to Lerwick and Aberdeen two hours later. This renewed a link with the past when the North Company had offered Norwegian sailings for 23 years until 1908. This service continued in June, July and August for the next three years with slight timetable adjustments.

Meanwhile, a report at this time suggested that a complete fleet replacement would cost around £100 million. Napier University suggested that using aluminium-constructed catamarans, each costing £40 million, would mean that up to 800 passengers and 100 cars could be carried, thereby saving up to two-thirds of the journey time to Shetland.

In 1993, investigative reports for Highlands and Islands Enterprise and Shetland Islands Council into more economic ways of providing ferry services to and from Aberdeen suggested that the Government provided and owned the ships, with P&O Scottish Ferries or others managing them.

TENDERING FOR THE ROUTES

In the summer of 1995, the Scottish Office invited companies to tender for the new contract to serve the Northern Isles but the west coast operator Caledonian MacBrayne was excluded from the tendering process. The General Election and change of Government in May 1997 led to delays in completing the tender process and on 24th July 1997, the new Secretary of State for Scotland, Donald Dewar MP confirmed that P&O Scottish Ferries had won the contract for a further five years in the face of competition from Sea Containers and Orkney Ferries. However, with the P&O vessels ageing, new Safety of Life at Sea (SOLAS) regulations being introduced (with which the ships did not comply) and Scottish devolution on the horizon, a new tendering process for the operation of the services beyond 2002 began almost immediately. This time around, Caledonian MacBrayne were able to participate with expressions of interest, and tenders were invited in summer 1998.

On 17th December 1999, the Scottish Executive, answerable to the Scottish Parliament on transport matters, announced that four companies – P&O Scottish Ferries, Serco/Denholm, Sea Containers and Caledonian MacBrayne and its partners – would be invited to submit tenders by March 2000 to operate the new contract. As part of their respective tenders, the participating companies were obliged to make public their plans for the future services. The P&O tender was initially based on acquisition of second-hand vessels for the Aberdeen

routes and engine upgrading/replacement on the *St. Ola*. The deadline was extended to the end of May 2000 during which time P&O revised their proposals to include new ships at a cost of around £100 million with the proposed vessels very similar to those, which subsequently appeared with NorthLink. The company appeared confident of continuing their association with the Northern Isles. The Serco/Denholm bid was based on a single passenger vessel operating on a 24-hour basis. Such a service – daytime one-way and overnight the other – would have been unlikely to meet the main customer requirement for an end of day departure and overnight crossing. Additionally, the timetable was tight and allowed no flexibility for bad weather or other delays. Meanwhile, Sea Containers withdrew from the bid process.

Caledonian MacBrayne anticipated growth on the routes, estimating around £8 million greater passenger revenue than P&O. They led a consortium that included the Royal Bank of Scotland, funders and owners of the new ships, the Isle of Wight ferry operator Wightlink, National Express and the shipbuilders Ferguson of Port Glasgow and Devon-based Appledore Shipyard. In the event, the final consortium was an equal partnership between CalMac and Royal Bank of Scotland with Wightlink and other partners having ended their interest prior to submission.

During a courtesy visit to Stromness by their *Clansman* on 31st January 2000, Caledonian MacBrayne gave details of the three new vessels they would provide if successful. Two large 12,000 gross ton, 24-knot ferries with capacity for 600 passengers would be built for the two Shetland routes with an 8,600-ton, 18+ knot, 600-passenger, 110-car ferry for the Pentland Firth crossing. The initial Expression of Interest was submitted on behalf of 'CalMac and Friends' then changed to 'CalMac NorthLink' and finally to 'NorthLink'. Further work was required on trading names for the new company, with Norlantic being one option. However, the name 'NorthLink' was subsequently adopted and continues to the present day.

On 5th October 2000, the Transport Minister Sarah Boyack MSP announced to the Scottish Parliament that the Caledonian MacBrayne partnership with Royal Bank of Scotland was the successful tender bid and that the new operation would begin in late 2002. For P&O Scottish Ferries it was the end of a long history serving Orkney and Shetland, but for Caledonian MacBrayne, it was a significant, if somewhat logical extension of their operations. NorthLink Orkney & Shetland Ferries was quickly established and with headquarters in Stromness, they set about ordering the promised car and passenger ferries, for introduction in October 2002. Although CalMac was a joint venture partner providing technical and ship management services, NorthLink was to be an otherwise autonomous business with its own staff, management and way of delivering services.

FAREWELL TO P&O

The last days of the P&O vessels were not trouble free. The *St. Clair* made her final sailing on 30th September 2002, operating the final northbound P&O Scottish Ferries sailing from Aberdeen to Lerwick. She sailed to Leith the next day and was subsequently sold to Saudi Arabian owners to be based in Jeddah for Pilgrim traffic on the Red Sea, under the name of the *Barakat*.

With the imminent arrival of NorthLink in October 2002 and the need for the pier at Stromness to be upgraded in advance of the new services, the *St. Sunniva* made her last call on 14th April 2002. Using Kirkwall for the remainder of her season, she paid off on 30th September 2002, operating the final 18.00 hrs departure from Lerwick to be replaced next day by the new ships. She sailed to Leith for lay-up and was sold to Al Thurya of Dubai for further trading as the *Faye*.

Meanwhile, on 30th September 2002, the *St. Ola*, under the command of Captain Willie Mackay, made her final sailing from Stromness to Stromness, prior to sailing to Leith and onwards to Estonian ferry operators Saaremaa Shipping Company. Her departure from Orkney brought to an end 110 years of continuous service of the four ships to bear the name *St. Ola*. The final sailing of the *St. Rognvald* for P&O Scottish Ferries took place on 28th September 2002, following which she was sold to Gulf Offshore of Aberdeen and chartered by the newly established Norse Island Ferries, continuing to serve Shetland for a time.

Top: The **St. Sunniva** *leaves Aberdeen on her midday sailing to Stromness and Lerwick. (Colin Smith)*

Above: The **St. Clair** *(ex* **Tregastel***) outward bound from Aberdeen on 26th June 2002. (Colin Smith)*

P&O FERRIES FLEET - OCTOBER 2012

	Gross Tonnage	Year Built	Speed (Knots)	Passengers	Cars/ Trailers	Route
BORE SONG	25,235	2011	19.0	12	210T	Middlesborough-Zeebrugge
EUROPEAN CAUSEWAY	20646	2000	22.5	410	315C	Larne-Cairnryan
EUROPEAN ENDEAVOUR	22152	2000	22.5	366	120L	Liverpool-Dublin
EUROPEAN HIGHLANDER	21128	2002	22.5	410	315C	Larne-Cairnryan
EUROPEAN SEAWAY	22986	1991	21.0	200	120L	Dover-Calais
EXPRESS	5902	1998	42.0	868	195C	Larne-Cairnryan/Troon
NORBANK	17464	1993	21.5	114	125T	Liverpool-Dublin
NORBAY	17464	1992	21.5	114	125T	Liverpool-Dublin
NORQUEEN	17884	1980	17.5	12	155T	Tilbury-Zeebrugge
NORSKY	19992	1999	20.0	12	194T	Middlesborough-Rotterdam
NORSTREAM	19992	1999	20.0	12	194T	Tilbury-Zeebrugge
PRIDE OF BRUGES	31598	1987	18.0	1050	310C	Hull-Zeebrugge
PRIDE OF BURGUNDY	28138	1992	21.0	1420	465C	Dover-Calais
PRIDE OF CALAIS	26433	1987	22.0	2290	585C	Due to be laid-up
PRIDE OF DOVER	26433	1987	22.0	2290	585C	Laid-up
PRIDE OF CANTERBURY	30635	1991	21.0	2000	537C	Dover-Calais
PRIDE OF HULL	59925	2001	22.0	1360	205C	Hull-Rotterdam
PRIDE OF KENT	30635	1992	21.0	2000	537C	Dover-Calais
PRIDE OF ROTTERDAM	59925	2000	22.0	1360	205C	Hull-Rotterdam
PRIDE OF YORK	31785	1987	18.0	1050	310C	Hull-Zeebrugge
SPIRIT OF BRITAIN	47592	2011	22.0	2000	194C	Dover-Calais
SPIRIT OF FRANCE	47592	2012	22.0	2000	194C	Dover-Calais

*The **Spirit of France** and **Spirit of Britain** at the Eastern Docks, Dover in September 2012. (John Hendy)*